STAND TALL

STAND TALL

FIGHTING FOR MY LIFE, INSIDE AND OUTSIDE THE RING

DEWEY BOZELLA

with Tamara Jones

ecco

An Imprint of HarperCollins*Publishers*

HarperCollins books may be purchased for educational, business, or sales promotional use. For information please e-mail the Special Markets Department at SPsales@harpercollins.com.

FIRST EDITION

Designed by Ashley Tucker

All photographs are from the author's collection.

Library of Congress Cataloging-in-Publication Data has been applied for.

ISBN 978-0-06-220815-6

16 17 18 19 20   OV/RRD   10 9 8 7 6 5 4 3 2 1

This book is dedicated to Trena and Diamond, the two people who are in my heart and soul for life. I love you.

A special dedication to J. Emma Crapser, who died unjustly. Through her, I learned morals, obligations, and responsibilities. And through her, I learned the importance of life, freedom, and death. J. Emma Crapser, may you be at peace, and God Bless You.

ACKNOWLEDGMENTS

I would like to thank Mickey Steiman and David Steinberg for their dedication and hard work on my case for my two trials. I know it has been a long journey of thirty-two years to prove my innocence. I have been blessed with the cooperation and support of the Innocence Project. They did a wonderful job of believing in me when all odds were against me. I am grateful for the hard work and dedication of Barry C. Scheck, Angela Amel, and Olga Akselrod. Together, they went above and beyond to secure my freedom. I would also like to thank Wilmer Cutler Pickering Hale and Dorr, based in New York City. I was blessed with the counsel of three exceptional lawyers: Peter J. Macdonald, Ross E. Firsenbaum, and Shauna Friedman, all of whom worked on my case for free. I'd like to thank them, and their staff, for helping me get back my freedom. Special thanks to Maura Mandt for having me at the ESPN ESPY Awards, where I was awarded the Arthur Ashe Award for Courage. That was one of the greatest moments of my life. I would also like to thank José Morales, who directed the ESPN film *26 Years: The*

Dewey Bozella Story. Special thanks to Beth Rasin for helping to start the Dewey Bozella Foundation, which has helped teenagers stay out of trouble out in the streets. Lastly, I want to thank everyone who helped bring this book into the world. Thank you, and God bless you all.

STAND TALL

PROLOGUE

I DON'T REMEMBER WHAT THE DAY MY LIFE DISAPPEARED LOOKED LIKE, whether there was snow on the ground or birds in the sky or boats on the river. I only saw it briefly as my guards led me in shackles from the transport van to the way station where the New York Department of Corrections sorts out its convicts before sending them on to their assigned prison. Reception, they call it. As if you were checking into a grand hotel where everyone calls you "sir" and the maids leave mints on your pillow. *What a strange word,* I thought, *to describe the process of becoming a prisoner.* It's not about being received at all. When you come right down to it, being locked up is about being officially rejected, returned like defective human merchandise to be inventoried, catalogued, and hidden away on an unreachable shelf. I shuffled up to the desk where a corrections officer was waiting for me. He had seen my picture in that morning's *Poughkeepsie Journal,* and now his eyes narrowed in recognition.

Oh, you the one murdered that little old lady! I willed my face to stay blank and waited for him to begin issuing his orders: first, I was to remove my belt and shoelaces. No explanation was offered or required: I knew they had me on suicide watch, and anything that I could conceivably loop around my throat to cut off my airway had to be considered a potential weapon. Taking your own life, in the prison system, is regarded as just another escape attempt, and they seal off all possible exits. I handed over the belt and laces and moved to the next station. *Oh, you the one!* The COs assigned to processing seemed to have been handpicked for their contempt, for their ability to send us into the prison system with a clear understanding that we were now subhuman. Every word, every procedure was filled with disgust, made rough by officers who knew exactly how far they could push without getting written up for abuse. I was patted down and strip-searched, every orifice peered into and probed, the eggy breath of the barking guards hot in my face. My thick hair was shorn to the scalp in a few hard swipes, and my mustache buzzed off in one. I was ordered to stand still, arms and legs spread, while officers sprayed me with sticky pesticide like a mangy dog off the street. I felt my humiliation build, shame sparking into anger, until every last nerve ending felt like a live wire. After hours of this debasement, I suddenly itched for someone to cross the line, to lay a hand on me so I could fight. *C'mon, just do it,* I silently willed them. I craved that small, calculated violence of knuckles against flesh, muscle to muscle, the simple fairness of raw strength versus raw strength. Fighting was my pain reliever. It was the only way I knew how to let out the anger and hate rotting me away from the inside like poison. There was a direct line running from my heart to my fists. Still electric and bristling, I changed into my newly issued prison greens. From there, it was medical tests all day long, poked and swabbed for TB, HIV, the clap, you name it. Finally, someone issued me my ID and spit out the number I was to commit to memory and recite back at head count three times a day: "84A0172. This is who you are." My name didn't matter anymore;

the person—the life—attached to it no longer existed. I was led back to a cell. I tossed my state-issued belongings on the bed and a small New Testament tumbled onto the lumpy inch-thin mattress. I opened it up to read. And that's when all hell broke loose.

Pure, uncut fear shot through me for the first time since hearing the word *guilty*. How in the hell was I going to deal with my sentence? Twenty years to life. To *life*. I could die behind bars, get buried in some potter's field, no one there to mourn me. I started bellowing like a crazed animal, ranting, screaming at no one, at anyone, at everyone.

"Why is this happening to me? What have I ever done to deserve twenty years to life? What have I done? I went to school! I was getting my shit together! I didn't do this! Yeah, I know I done wrong before, but I ain't never murdered anybody. I did not kill anyone. Man, fuck everybody. I don't care about life. I don't trust nobody. Nobody. Fuck the world! Fuck everyone. God, too." I threw the New Testament hard across the tiny room. "How'm I supposed to deal with this?" I spent my first night as 84A0172 with my mind twisting around this new reality, trying to find some reassuring surface to grip, only to fall, again and again, back into the dark well. By morning, I was spent, the panic replaced by a new kind of flatness, the dull resolve of a fighter who knows he's lost but wills himself to stay standing no matter what. I was herded into a van and delivered to Sing Sing Correctional Facility. The bored CO doing the paperwork sifted through my bag of belongings, writing down what I could and could not have. He gestured to my surrendered pile of civilian clothes.

"What do you want done with this? Send it home, burn it, or give it away?"

"I ain't got nobody to send it to," I told him. "I got life. Do whatever you want with it."

1

YOU HAVE TO TRAIN YOUR MIND FOR A LIFETIME IN PRISON. You've got to shadowbox with your heart, or you might slip down a hole you'll never climb out of. I've seen that happen to people. Survival is all about conditioning yourself, body and mind. When you're a fighter, you tend to look at life from that perspective. I never lost a bout when I stepped into the ring, but the Fourth of July was another story. Holidays don't mean shit to a man in prison. Christmas, Thanksgiving, maybe you get a little something extra to eat at chow, but otherwise you're just looking at another day with the same number of hours to dissolve away in slow motion, nothing special about that. I wasn't one of those Hollywood movie cons who scratched hash marks in the cinder-block walls to keep track of how many days or months or years had gone by. I didn't want to remember what a Christmas tree smelled like, or how fine the sisters looked in their colorful Easter dresses. Practice made me pretty good at forgetting what day it was, never giving emotion an opening to sneak up on me and land a haymaker. But Independence Day ambushed me in my cell at Sing Sing.

Sing Sing hunches over the Hudson River like a gloomy old fortress atop its rocky ridge just thirty-five miles north of New York City, which is where I was born and not so much raised as released, left to run wild on the streets, either dodging trouble or making it. I've been a case number for most of my life as far as the State of New York is concerned. Foster care, at-risk programs, welfare checks, jail—the sorry but predictable path in my time for an African American kid who'd lost his parents, his home, and all reason to believe any other life was waiting for him. So what. Lots of people go through tough times. Don't get me wrong: I'm not feeling sorry for myself. You might be surprised to hear that I consider myself blessed. I made my choices, and my mistakes, and I own them. I tell every kid I meet now not to be as stupid as I was. But I still can't help wondering sometimes what might have happened to that cast-off child I was, if love had been part of the equation, if things had been different, if God's plan for me hadn't been so damn complicated. I'm fifty-six years old now and still working on the puzzle.

On the Fourth of July at Sing Sing, the cellblocks facing the Hudson would go ape after lockdown when the fireworks began going off over the water from whatever nearby park or town happened to be putting on a show. From my cell on the backside of the sprawling prison complex, I could hear the distant cracks and muffled booms of the fireworks, accompanied by the whooping and hollering of the luckier inmates who had a view through their barred windows: *Yo, yo, yo! Oh, shiiit, man, look at that! Man, that's crazy! You see that shit?* I couldn't decide whether it was funny or sad that Independence Day was the one holiday you didn't have to be actually free to be a part of. Man, did I envy those cats with the view in the front galleries on the top tiers. I looked out onto nothing but more prison—concrete and dirt—for a good deal of that time. I was four years into my bid when my chance to move to the front finally came.

You have to wonder why a man denied justice would want to celebrate the democracy that failed him so miserably, but there I was, gazing through the bars on my cell window like an excited kid on that first Fourth I could see. I watched in silence for a good ten minutes as the fiery fountains and starbursts exploded in bright color against the night. Beauty is so rare in prison that you take it in in gulps when you have it, until you make yourself sick.

THE SIGHT OF FIREWORKS AFTER SO LONG reeled my mind back to childhood, me running around all day with my little brothers and our homeboys, all of us hyper and happy and full of piss. Fourth of July was one of those holidays you didn't need a nice home or lot of money to celebrate: it belonged to everybody. New York always pulled out all the stops, and whether you were in the projects or Park Avenue, you got the same sky. My neighborhood off Murdock Avenue in St. Albans, Queens, was full of working-class families, and there were always big, rowdy block parties on the Fourth, music blasting, everyone eating BBQ, drinking beer and cans of pop icy from the cooler, getting along and having a good time. I spent weeks getting my pocket money together so I could buy some cherry bombs or a couple of Roman candles or a box of dynamite-stick firecrackers, with enough left over for some candy to carefully ration over the long, busy day I had laid out with my younger brothers Ernie and Albert, the ones closest to me in age. We were tight like that. And we had big plans for the Fourth of July. Those little sizzle-stick things? Sparklers? Not for us, man. No way. The Murdock Avenue boys meant business.

Yo, yo check this out! We started off small, just blowing up soda cans. They delivered a decent little blast, with enough flying shards of aluminum to make a twelve-year-old drunk on danger. Bottles worked, too. The thrill wore off too fast, though, and we boldly moved on to mailboxes, which offered only a muffled thud but were still entertaining for the hit-and-run element involved. From there, we graduated with cocky confidence to neighbors' garbage cans. The plastic ones were disappointing, but we quickly learned that a couple of cherry bombs could reliably blow a metal one to kingdom come, like something out of a war movie, with the kind of teeth-rattling force that made us go from taunting *nah, nah cherry bomb* to screaming *Oh, SHIT!* as we hightailed it down the street while some raging grown-up charged after us: *Get away from my yard, damn kids!* I remember feeling reckless and badass, and, for a little knucklehead kid, powerful.

Once we'd had our fill of detonating inanimate objects like some marauding band of grade-school guerrillas, we would thread our way through the crowds milling on the street or gathered in the park. By then we were loopy on sugar and adrenaline. We'd snatch a firecracker from the twenty-packs we wore like ammo belts, light the fuse, then just randomly throw it into a knot of unsuspecting people and wait for it to go off at their feet. Every now and then, we hit the Powerball, and some dude would grab his smoldering butt. We threw them at each other, too. Never aimed for the face, just the butt and legs. *Yo, man, yo my butt is on fire!* We laughed till we doubled over and the tears were rolling down our faces. Soda cans to bottles to mailboxes to garbage cans to each other. That was how the law of the jungle worked on the Fourth of July.

Twenty years to life. That's how it worked in Sing Sing. Bitterly I turned away from the grimy window in my six-by-ten-foot cell.

I don't even want to watch the damn fireworks no more, I told myself. I struggled to shove the happy memories back into their lockbox, to reclaim the numbness that was my default setting: *Aight, just treat it as another day. Holidays don't mean shit, man.*

I had forgotten my own cardinal rule and had to pay now with self-pity: look with your eyes, I reminded myself, never your heart.

The sky fell silent and dark again, and I pushed away Dewey Bozella, the little kid laughing until his sides hurt, and lay down on my narrow iron bed, falling asleep the same way I had for thousands of nights past and would for thousands more to come, as inmate number 84A0172. Convicted murderer. There's no way ever to take the sharp edge off those words or grow accustomed to their pain. Especially when they're a lie, when you're paying for another man's crime, your whole life hijacked by people who turned their backs on the truth. That they did it so casually made it all the worse. I wasn't the victim of some grand conspiracy or complicated setup: I was a convenient scapegoat for an ambitious prosecutor and a bumbling police department. The course of my entire life would change in their hands. All it took was one word.

Guilty.

That one word did what no fighter in the ring ever could: brought me to my knees, howling in agony, sobbing so hard I could barely breathe, disbelief hardening into a despair as vast and deep as a winter ocean turned to ice. There was no one in the courtroom to console me or hug me before deputies led me away in handcuffs. No family or friends had come to my brief, sorry trial. I was as alone as alone can get. "I didn't do it!" I wailed again and again. I'm not going to lie; I was never anyone's goody-goody, and I had been on a self-destructive road since I was in grade school. I had gotten into trouble before and had a short rap sheet for stealing. I took bicycles left outside grocery stores. I took boom boxes. I took a wallet from a guy on the street one time. But I never took anyone's life.

In that Poughkeepsie courtroom, on December 3, 1983, though, the State of New York took mine.

By the time I arrived at Sing Sing at the beginning of 1984, the world's most notorious maximum-security prison was housing some two thousand felons. I was twenty-three years old, and it would take longer than I had already lived to prove I didn't belong there.

THE WHOLE SORRY MESS BEGAN YEARS BEFORE I ACTUALLY LANDED IN SING SING, though, on an ordinary Thursday morning in June 1977. I had just gotten released on my own recognizance for stealing a $250 stereo down in New York City, and no sooner had I left that courtroom than along came a pair of cops to arrest me all over again. Like I said, I'll be the first to admit that I was no choirboy, so I can't say I was all that surprised to be crossways with the police. At the time, I was an eighteen-year-old high school dropout who'd been heading toward a life of crime for a while already—stealing shit, smoking reefer, drinking, gambling, hooking up with women much older and more troubled than I'd ever be. Relocating from the city to Poughkeepsie and moving in with my older half brother, Tony, was supposed to be a fresh start, but my efforts to turn my life around and get on the right path were hit-and-miss so far, and the local cops already had me in their scopes as trouble imported from NYC. I'd only been in town for a couple of months, but I'd made myself a fixture in Mansion Square Park, a favorite gathering spot for sketchy homeboys who were generally up to nothing good. Drinking and gambling were my preferred pastimes at Mansion Square Park, and I was still dabbling in petty crime, too, still stealing bikes and stereos when an easy opportunity arose. I'd already gotten busted in Poughkeepsie once on a larceny charge that didn't stick. But part of me did want more out of life than the streets, and I'd lined up a low-level job on a construction site so maybe I could learn carpentry, have a trade. I was on my way to the site that summer morning when the cops cuffed me.

Awww, shit, I thought to myself.

"You're under arrest," one of the cops said.

"What for?" I demanded, taking a quick mental inventory of what I'd lifted of late.

"Murder."

I laughed.

"*Murder?*" I scoffed. This was a joke, some kind of lame-ass scare tactic. "Murder? You got the wrong man. I didn't kill nobody. I don't know what you're talking about."

They hauled me in for questioning. I expected to be out in an hour tops. I hadn't done anything, so I knew there was no way they had any evidence linking me to any crime, let alone homicide. No evidence, no charges, right? I was a cocky teenager back then, thought I knew all about handling myself with the law, but in truth, I was naive as hell. This was a mistake, I reasoned, and the truth would set me free. God's own words. I didn't belong to a church or lead a righteous life then, but that much I had faith in. I clung to the truth like a trusty life raft.

Back at the station, the detectives took me into an interview room and turned on a tape recorder.

"Tell us how you killed her."

"Man, I ain't telling you shit," I snarled back. I picked up the tape recorder and threw it across the room, shattering it. Whatever game they were playing with me, it was no longer funny.

The detectives pressed harder, demanding to know why I had tortured a helpless old woman, murdered her in her own home, and for what? What was it, a robbery she walked in on? Where had I been on the night of June 14? Had I been in Mansion Square Park with a kid named Wayne Moseley?

I tried to think back ten days. I vaguely remembered Moseley being around one afternoon we were playing basketball. I remembered that that was the night I stayed there too late shooting dice and drinking and missed the last bus home to Tony's apartment in Beacon. I had cajoled some kid who was watching the game into giving me his ten-speed bike, saying I was going to get us all some beer and would be right back. Sucker just handed it over to me, and I rode it home, wobbling all the way. I felt bad about it the next day and rode the bike back to the park to return it, but the kid hadn't shown up again.

That wasn't what happened, the detectives insisted. They said that I had walked the few blocks to Emma Crapser's house with some other teen thugs, broke in through the front door, then suffocated her when she walked in on the burglary, that I tortured and killed a ninety-two-year-old white woman.

"Man, I'm not trying to hear that shit!" I exploded. "I didn't do that."

By now, I was going off like an idiot. Why were they accusing me? What had I done to make them accuse me of murder? Where was the evidence? And how do you prove your innocence when your alibi is that you were sweet-talking a bike off somebody whose name you didn't know and drunk-riding it home? Tony had spent the night at his girlfriend's and didn't see me till the next day.

"We got you," said the lead detective, Lieutenant Art Regula. "We finally got your ass."

They took me, cursing my head off, down to central booking at the county jail. First thing I saw was a KKK poster on the wall, right there in the open: WE'RE LOOKING FOR KLANSMEN, it said. Right there on the goddamn wall in the county jail. I knew then that I was in for it. They held me for twenty-eight days, brazenly violating civil rights that I had no means to protect—other than hollering that it wasn't fair—knowing even at eighteen that three days was the maximum you could be held without charges. The guards menaced me on a daily basis, vowing to "come in there and fuck you up," to give the "one who murdered that old lady" what he deserved. I had heard of dudes having their arms broken in that jail, of beat-downs and suspicious suicides. I put on a tough demeanor, but inside, I was scared shitless. Nobody on the outside had come looking for me, nobody had my back, nobody would even miss me. I had been disposable my whole life, and now I was a black kid suspected of murdering a white grandma, in the custody of KKK-recruiting cops. I figured it wasn't a matter of whether they would come for me, but when.

Inmates could be out of their cells for blocks of time during the day, to watch TV in the common room, or play cards or whatever. One day, when the tension had grown unbearable, I refused orders to lock back into our cells. If I was in that little cell, I was cornered and could be stomped by the officers who had been threatening to avenge Emma Crapser's murder on their own terms. I took my mattress and laid it down. I would need the bed frame as a possible weapon, and the thin mattress could serve as my shield. Then I got the cleaning supplies left on the gallery for inmates to mop down their cells. I broke the broomstick in half to use as a club, and laid the mop next to it, thinking how the metal wringer on the handle could cause some damage, crack a guard's plastic shield, if I swung it like a big hammer. The bottle of floor wax would come in handy, too. *Bring it, motherfuckers,* I thought, *just bring it.*

"Lock in!" the guards ordered everyone.

"I'm not gonna let you all just beat me up," I shouted back. "You wanna bring it, bring it. I'm not locking in, man."

The other inmates stayed outside their cells, too, egging me on, raising the stakes from refusing an order to inciting a riot if the guards came back.

"Lock in!"

This time, the other inmates obeyed the order. I was on my own. I emptied the bottle of floor wax, grabbed my mattress shield, and ran to the back of the gallery.

"Yo, man, you little fucking bastard!" A guard had discovered my floor-wax moat. If I was going to get an ass-whipping, they were going to bust their own asses first. They sent back an officer named Lopez to talk me down. Lopez had been cool with me, and eventually I realized I had no choice but to trust him when he swore that he wouldn't let the COs come back and beat me. He was good to his word, but I lived on constant edge waiting for my arraignment.

I finally went before a judge in late July. The prosecutor had no evidence or testimony to present. The case was instantly dismissed, but the injustice of it all followed me home, anyway.

"Listen, man, you gotta leave. I can't be around this murder thing," Tony told me when I showed up. He had made no attempt to visit me or try to help when I got arrested, and I half wondered now but didn't dare ask if he actually thought I had had anything to do with the crime. Tony was much older than I was and had been out of my life for years. We were just starting to build a relationship, and we couldn't have been more different. He was as country as I was city slick, and my brush with the law over a grisly, headlining crime made him nervous. Tony was about to sign a new lease and set up house with his girlfriend, and he had a job he liked, working with at-risk kids at the Division of Youth. He wasn't willing to bet his stability on the reputation of a brother he scarcely knew. Kicking me out was an easy choice. Thing is, I was so used to people turning their backs on me by that time, it didn't bother me all that much. I'd lived on the streets before, and I could do it again.

The failure to deliver an indictment against me in the Crapser murder should have been the end of the whole ugly episode, but it was just the beginning. When you're eighteen years old, you think the world is yours for the taking, ripening like a piece of fruit on the vine; you think you have more tomorrows than you can count. You think that you could become a major-league baseball player, or a movie star like Chuck Norris. That someday you'll be the man, driving a new car and coming home to a beautiful wife and a big house full of children who idolize you. You don't imagine yourself falsely convicted, locked up, left to rot. But six years later, that's exactly where I found myself. Inmate number 84A0172. Return address, Sing Sing. And still they had no evidence.

BEHIND BARS, I WAS JUST ONE MORE VOICE in a constant background chorus of men proclaiming they were the innocent victims of an unjust system. I knew the din would swallow my shouts of rage before they ever left my throat. So I made the only choice that was wholly mine left to make: I locked my soul up, too. Sealing my true self up tight—putting my soul in solitary—was the only way I could see to survive this terrifying underworld that was my new home. Back then, someone with a life sentence was automatically stripped of the civil rights most Americans take for granted, the ones my enslaved ancestors fought to the death for. I couldn't vote. I couldn't marry. Couldn't own property, apply for a loan, buy an insurance policy, or do anything else that required signing a binding contract. I was civilly dead. A goddamn walking zombie. I was just like the three pairs of green trousers and six pairs of white socks and single bar of soap issued to me, property of the State of New York, with a value next to nothing. Fuck that shit.

For the first few months, I just stayed to myself. Cell R-31 was on the second tier of B block, which stretched out like a nightmare circus train packed with caged men, bars as far as the eye could see, 618 cells spanning the distance of two football fields. B block was where all the new inmates initially went, separated from the general population while they supposedly "adjusted" to prison life. They were in the process of some kind of renovation when I got there, and the wall back where I was had been torn down, replaced by plywood boards with gaps where the snow came through. I spent my first night there shivering beneath the thin single blanket as the winter wind and snow blew in through the makeshift wall.

The year before I got there, B block had been the scene of a fifty-three-hour riot by inmates who held nineteen guards hostage before releasing them unharmed. B block still bristled with leftover hostilities and riot scores waiting to be settled. Tension was always a given in the cellblocks, called galleries, and prisoners outnumbered staff by more than two to one. When the state conducted its investigation into the 1983 uprising, the two-hundred-page report

it issued pointed out that the majority of corrections officers dealing directly with inmates had less than a year's experience as a CO,
and every single one of them had put in for a transfer by the end
of their first day on the job at Sing Sing. There were always more
newjacks than veteran COs. That kind of inexperience makes both
the staff and inmates jumpy. You never knew what might go down,
or whether the COs would be able to stop it from escalating. No
way could you rely on them to keep you safe. First week I was in
Sing Sing, I had run into an inmate I recognized. Slim had been in
one of the group foster homes with me as a kid. He was doing time
for robbery now. Inmates usually don't tell each other why they're
there—it's nobody's business, and you don't want to become a target for some snitch working a deal with prosecutors. I knew that
even if I kept my mouth shut, my charges were unlikely to remain
private. Torturing and killing an old woman would rank right down
there in the scum bucket with rapists and child predators. Marked
men, all. The ones who get jumped and beaten to a pulp or sliced
across the face. The COs were the ones to generally put the word
out: *That's the motherfucker raped that little boy!* I wouldn't go so far
as to say Slim and I were actually friends, but he was as close to that
as I had then, and I was grateful to have a potential ally if I needed
one. No more than a week after we reconnected, though, Slim got
himself killed by another inmate. I never heard what the beef was,
but the swift violence of the place unnerved me. A week after Slim
died, I saw a dude get stabbed in the eye. And I mean right through
the eyeball. No idea what he did, or who did it to him, it happened
that fast. *Shit,* I thought. *I ain't takin' no shit in here. Dude even
comes close to me, I'll throw down with him.* Your life was always in
danger. I knew from the outset that I was going to have to develop
my own security plan. In prison, brute strength isn't what will keep

you from getting stabbed up when the shit hits. Your mind will save you before your muscles do.

My nature is to be on the quiet side unless I'm threatened, so it was easy just to stay to myself, blend in, and watch while I tried to get a sense of my new home. I would pretend to be watching TV or listening to music with a group of guys during rec, but really I was studying them, figuring out Sing Sing's unwritten prisoners' code and who wielded the most power. I never sat down, and I kept my back to the wall. Gang members often controlled the phones, and if you didn't know anybody or have money to pay them off, you wouldn't get your turn. I didn't have anyone to call, anyway, so that was a beef I could easily avoid. You could also get jumped or find yourself stuck in the throat if you changed the channel on the block's communal television without permission from the prisoner currently in charge. The violence didn't surprise me, but something else I quickly observed about Sing Sing did. Man, that place is *loose*. Anything you could get on the street, you could get inside, no problem. And the COs didn't just look the other way; plenty of them were in on the action. Four guards and a sergeant had been indicted on corruption charges the year before I got there, but the party went on, from what I could tell, earning Sing Sing its nickname, Swing Swing. It was wilder than the old Times Square.

The code among inmates boiled down to one simple unbreakable rule: Mind your own damn business if you don't want to get hurt, and respect everyone until they disrespect you. You accidentally bump a guy in line or walking to the yard, you stop, meet his eye, and say "excuse me, man" like you mean it, or you may feel a shiv jammed into your gut next time you pass his man Trini. If you're out walking on the gallery, you make sure to keep your eyes straight ahead and never look into another man's cell. Different galleries were known for different activities. J and N galleries offered prostitution during the day shift, and L and P galleries took over the sex trade at night. If you weren't pimping or partaking, you stayed away and let the others do their thing. The yard was a drug bazaar. Then you had the covert food concessions run by felons with a culinary talent. If you wanted to gamble, there was 21 and blackjack and poker in M gallery. In prison, cigarettes are the basic currency. You can even turn packs of cigarettes into cash, which is forbidden but necessary for certain illicit transactions. At the commissary, smokes were a dollar a pack in the early '80s, but not everyone had money in their canteen accounts—some had it garnished because they owed the state money, and others didn't have any family or people on the outside to deposit the funds allowed. That was my situation early on. But say you have a pack of cigarettes. Here's how the hustle works: You trade the one-dollar pack for two bags of chips and a soda that would have cost you a buck fifty in the canteen. You're already ahead fifty cents, but then you can sell those chips and soda for whatever the market will bear— either bartering for more items, or getting more cash from some hungry inmate who was on keep-lock and had lost his commissary privileges. If you have a carton of cigarettes, you can really make out, selling seven packs for ten dollars. You can then take that ten dollars (or the equivalent in cigarettes) and give it to the female CO moonlighting in the back of J gallery, and that's how you get sex. This is what ten dollars can get you in Swing Swing:

Two sticks of reefer, or a bag of dope

Blow job from a female CO

Five pieces of raw chicken stolen from the mess hall's walk-in refrigerator

As for me, I was down for the reefer or the chicken dinner, but mess with a CO? Forget it. There were some lady guards who weren't half bad-looking and all, even though prison rules specifically banned them from wearing makeup or perfume or anything that might be seen as "enticing" to the inmates. I had never lacked for female companionship on the outside and had been living with a woman I'll call Stephanie and her little girl before getting sent away; it was as close to settled down as I'd ever been, and it had given me a feel for what being part of a real family might be like. There were trailers for conjugal visits at Sing Sing, but that was only for married couples, and back in 1983, you still couldn't get married while incarcerated if you had a murder conviction. Despite my sorry reality, I knew that hooking up with a female officer, even in a quick, strictly business transaction, was stupid. She could set you up at the drop of a hat. Aside from that, if anything went down—someone's cell getting tossed and his bank or his dope confiscated, or a weapon found—you would immediately be seen as a likely snitch. And suspicion of rat is the same as confirmation of rat in a place like Sing Sing. Gonna get you jumped either way.

The constant dirty gray light, the jingle of keys and *clank clank clank* of cell doors being locked one by one, the smell of a thousand men all remind you every minute even through your sleep that you're in prison. That, and the loneliness. Right from the start, I felt more imprisoned by my own emotions than by the bars on my cell. I was always waiting for things that never materialized. A visit, a letter, a package. I thought about people on the outside all the time—my brothers, friends, Stephanie and her baby daughter, whom I'll call Angie. Stephanie was a year older than I was, a single mom who was trying to get her life together. She had a job at IBM and was going to community college. We met in line at the store.

Angie was just six months old when I moved in, and she considered me her father. I used to carry her around in my arms, change her diaper, push her in the stroller when Stephanie and I took her out for some fresh air. We'd known each other for nearly four years when I got convicted. She came to see me when I was being held downstate, before getting processed to Sing Sing. I remember being so damn glad to see her, how it just made my day.

"I have an appeal in," I told her excitedly. "Things may—"

"Dewey," she interrupted. "I gotta tell you something."

I felt my heart dive. She was going to tell me she was leaving me.

"Dewey, I had an abortion."

"What you mean?" I cried out. "You mean to fucking tell me you killed the only thing I had left in my life?" The only thing worse than my anger in that moment was my pain. "Girl or boy?" I demanded.

"Girl," she said, crying.

I looked at her and saw she was lying. It had been a son.

We held on to each other, though, and she wrote me in Sing Sing, promising to visit. I was there for three months before she finally showed up, her chatter about Angie and how fast she was growing falling over me like a shaft of sunlight. She promised to come back the next week. The day I was expecting her, I got up, showered, and dressed in clothes that had been cleaned by an inmate who worked in the prison laundry. You put your clothes in with the general population laundry, they were going to come back dingier than they went in, all mixed in with you didn't want to know what. But give the laundry dude a pack of cigarettes, he'd do your clothes separately on the side, deliver them back clean and neatly folded. I wanted to look my best for Stephanie. I waited to be called to the visiting room. Hours passed. She never showed. At mail call, I'd have correspondence from my lawyers now and then, and once in a while, a letter from her. *The baby's good,* she'd write, *I miss you, sorry I didn't make it, I'll be there next week.* Only she wasn't. It was tearing me apart.

One day, I was in the yard when I heard someone call my name: "Dewey!" I turned, but no one was there. No long after, it happened again. "Yo, Dewey, look out, look out!" I wheeled around, hands up, ready to fight. No one again. It was as if I had just gotten a preview of what could happen if I let my sentence stake a claim on my sanity. *This has got to stop, I'm not going to bug out.* I had to stay focused on the here and now. I made an important decision: I had to let everybody go, in my mind, had to get rid of them, turn my heart to ice. If I didn't get rid of the people I cared for, I was just going to get hurt. I had to let them go in order to do my time. I'd rather deal with loneliness than anticipation.

When Stephanie showed up again six months after her first visit, I was cold as hell to her in the visiting room. Gave her a quick hug, no kiss. I asked how Angie was doing. Then I told her straight up: "You gotta go. I gotta cut you off. I got to do my bid."

"What do you mean?" she asked, hurt and confused.

"Move on with your life. Do what you gotta do, but don't come back."

Stephanie was crying, saying she didn't understand why I was being like this.

"I don't even have a year in," I reminded her. "I don't want to be thinking about when you're going to come visit."

I left her sitting there at the table and walked through the door. The CO followed me out. "Listen, man, she's sitting there waiting for you," he urged me.

"Tell her I'm not coming back."

Back in my cell, I had to fight back tears of my own. I told myself it would hurt less to let it go. *Let it go, Dewey, let it go, let it go.*

IN PRISON, YOU DON'T HAVE FRIENDS. You have associates. Associates are who you hang out with. I didn't allow anybody to be a friend. It was safer that way. I had limited experience trusting folks as it was, so doing away with trust altogether was no big sacrifice on my part. I had learned back in juvie, though, that guys who didn't prove that they were willing to fight from the beginning would be turned into male prostitutes. First, they'd become a "Maytag," slang for the ones being broken into servitude by being forced to wash the underwear of whoever was tormenting them. It only got more degrading after that. My moment of truth came one day when someone did something wrong on the gallery, and the inmates who were outside were called back in as a result. I had nothing to do with it, but I was the first person one of the bigger guys saw as they came back in, and I got jumped. Next time I spotted the bully with his back turned, I was lucky enough to also spot a shovel discarded nearby, and I cracked him with it. Show no mercy, otherwise you become a victim. I sent the message loud and bloody clear that day that I would be no one's victim. I carried that attitude with me to Sing Sing.

I quickly established my own routine: get up at 6 A.M., get ready for breakfast, eat at 7, come back for chores—I was a porter, responsible for cleaning the gallery. Then I'd go out to the yard. The yard back then was a big field of grass and dirt. In one corner, people would lift weights. There were tables where guys might play chess or cards or just talk. There were hoops for basketball, a handball court, and a diamond for playing baseball. Babe Ruth himself had once played there and hit a record-smashing homer. It was back in 1929, long before major-league players had powerful agents and big endorsements; they used to make extra cash playing exhibition games. The Yanks came to Sing Sing to take on the inmate team—"The Black Sheep"—and Babe sent the ball flying over the prison wall, a reported 620 feet. What I wouldn't have given to see that.

I didn't socialize much early on, but one slim Spanish guy didn't take that as a snub. Jose was a talker, and I guess a fresh pair of ears was too good for him to pass up, so he just kept coming up to me in the yard, shooting the breeze like we were buddies, until finally, it seemed, we were. I liked his style. We traded stories about what we did on the streets, the girls we'd been with, that kind of bull jive. We smoked a fair amount of reefer together. That and the homemade prune wine some enterprising dudes sold out of their cells kept me in a welcome fog that blurred the glare of my day-to-day life. Nothing really mattered anymore. I watched the different prison dramas unfold from my safe distance—the deadly gang rivalries between the Bloods and the Latin Kings, the seething hatred of the small tight band of white supremacists, the high-stakes drug trafficking by the Colombians who considered being locked up just a way to get the state to pay for security while they continued running their outside business as usual. Even rogue operators were in constant danger. I remember a guy named Roscoe who was acting like a tough ass, trying to bully everyone, and one day he's out there lifting weights and gets a weight cracked over his head. My attitude came down to this: *As long as you leave me alone, I don't care if you want to kill someone else. Go ahead.* I did not care. I had set my automatic cruise control and fully intended to let the next twenty years to life pass in this state of blankness.

MY SURVIVAL PLAN WORKED FINE FOR A COUPLE OF YEARS, until I was coming in from the yard one day, through the long tunnel leading back to the flats—the ground floor of the cellblock—and all of a sudden, everything went quiet. When that stillness fell, you knew something bad had happened.

I kept walking through the tunnel, minding the unspoken code, eyes ahead. Then I saw him: some dude lying on the floor, leaking bad. All stabbed up, in a spreading pool of blood. Young black guy with ten, twenty holes in him or better. Had to have just happened, too. No alarms or COs running with a stretcher. I didn't feel like walking around him. *Fuck it,* I said to myself, and I stepped over him and kept on my way.

Back in my cell, it hit me, what I had just done. Hit me so hard I was shaking. *That was a human being back there, man,* the voice inside my head railed at me. *You walked right over him. Not even around him, man, right fucking over him. You didn't even give a shit. What have you become?* The voice wouldn't let up. I had fallen right into what the prison system is all about.

Who are you?

2

MURDER HAS BEEN A RECURRING PART OF MY LIFE SINCE I WAS NINE YEARS OLD.
It's a hard story for me to tell: first, because it hurts even now; and,
second, because so many crucial details of my own history were
kept from me. My childhood comes down to a faded patchwork of
mismatched pieces from my own memory and the scraps of truth,
lies, and misinformation everyone else gave me. For me, the real
starting point is when I was nine years old. Nine is when everything
changed.

I remember the house we were living in then, a corner lot with
a yard, in a mostly black neighborhood of Brooklyn. My mother,
Sandra, was dark skinned and, from what I can remember, beautiful. She had six of us kids, stair-stepped one after the other. Janice
was the oldest, followed by me. Then came Ernie, Albert, Michael,
and Leon. Our father's name was Albert Rader Bozella, but he went
by Harry. "Dirty Harry" was the name I secretly gave him. He was a
white man who wore glasses. I don't know what he did for a living,
but we weren't busted. We always ate and had clothes on our backs
and toys under the tree at Christmas. I suppose we were happy

enough, as long as Dirty Harry wasn't around. Dirty Harry didn't live with us full-time, which was a small mercy, because when he drove up and parked his boat of a black sedan at the curb, we all went into high alert. I would run and hide from him, trying to make myself invisible, but Dirty Harry had a hair-trigger temper, and it only made him madder if I didn't come when he hollered. Folks see the nasty scar I have on the back of my head now, they assume I got it in prison, or in some street fight before I got locked up. My father is the one who gave me that scar. It came from a baseball bat when I was eight.

The happier memories I have of those years, that place, all revolve around my brothers. We were inseparable, a crazy tumbleweed of commotion, always blowing through the quiet suburban streets on bikes, homemade go-carts, hijacked shopping carts, or whatever else we could find with a couple of wheels. We would spend hours prowling the woods that backed up to our neighborhood, trying to catch snakes or hunting squirrels with our slingshots. I was a very active kid, to put it mildly, and I was always into something. With me leading the charge, there is no question that the Bozella boys raised more than our fair share of hell, but our mother wasn't one to whip her children, and we knew it. The whole world had a more laid-back quality to it then. Nobody was ever warning us about child molesters or school shooters or any of that craziness kids have to worry about now. It was the 1960s, and everybody kept their doors open. The neighborhood kids migrated from one house to the next, and anyone's mom was everyone's mom. I remember our neighbor Miss Anne being so attached to Leon that you were as likely to find him clinging to her as to our own mother. As for me, I didn't take to people the same way Leon did with his baby's charm and sweet, open face. The difference between Leon at four years old and me at eight was the difference between a Christmas puppy and a feral dog. There was something still pure and unruined about Leon. Dirty Harry had made me slow to trust, and while I wouldn't call myself shy, I did prefer to watch the grown-up world from a safe distance. I wanted adults' approval, for sure, but I didn't expect to win it and wasn't sure I could pay for it. Pride was my downfall from the time I was old enough to say the word *no*.

I don't remember ever liking, much less loving, Dirty Harry. I never even sat down to dinner with him. I think of him as a slave owner. Why my mother was with him is something I'll never know, because he kept her down more than he ever helped her out. He was always hollering, thundering around the house like a charging bull, enraged by the whole sorry lot of us. Mom took the brunt of it, always getting smacked around no matter how hard she tried to appease him. But even then, I can't always reconcile how I want to think of her with what I remember. My first impulse is to say that Mom always protected us kids from Dirty Harry, that she made sure this madman never put his hands on us. But then the scar on the back of my head tells another story. I have no recollection of what I did to set Dirty Harry off that day—it could have been anything from roughhousing with Albert and Ernie to not picking up some toy, or even just looking at him wrong—but I remember my father had forced me to strip naked and was getting ready to whip me. He ordered me to come to him, but I ran instead. He picked up a baseball bat and threw it at my head, splitting my scalp open. I bolted out the door, butt-assed naked into the snow, clutching a dress of my sister's that I had snatched from the laundry on my way out. I stood there shivering in the street, blood running down my neck. My mother appeared at the door, trying to coax me inside.

"Dewey, come in, you're going to freeze," she pleaded.

"Not until he leaves," I cried.

She eventually prevailed over me, and Dirty Harry, and I folded myself half frozen into her warm arms. I would've given anything to have loved and felt loved by a father even half as much as I loved and felt loved by my mother.

Maybe we looked like a regular family to everybody else, but I think the neighbors must have known. My mother's women friends, like Miss Anne, didn't come around to visit when Dirty Harry's car was at the curb. There was something always different about us: a family in the strictly segregated 1960s in which a white man was married to a dark woman with their light-skinned kids in a black neighborhood. My first inkling that we weren't Dirty Harry's only family came when I was nine, and my mother, heavily pregnant with her seventh child, summoned me to her one warm afternoon when we were in the backyard. Dirty Harry was grilling a chicken I had watched run headless around our yard after he butchered it.

"Dewey, I have something to tell you," my mother said. "I want you to know you got another brother and three sisters. They're going to be coming and living with us real soon. I want you to take care of them. Will you promise to take care of your brothers and sisters for me?"

I listened, astonished by the news. I nodded excitedly.

"I will," I told her. "I promise."

It didn't dawn on me at that age to ask who these sudden siblings were, where they had been, or why they were moving in now. And I likewise didn't wonder where four extra people were going to sleep in our modest house. The backstory didn't matter to me; I just waited for them to appear. My sister, Janice, would probably welcome some more girls in the house, and a spare brother would strengthen the ranks if any of us needed backup in a schoolyard beef. As for Dirty Harry, he didn't say a word to us kids about these other kids of his, and we knew instinctively not to ask him any questions.

A couple of days after my mother's announcement, I came home from school and saw Dirty Harry's car outside. I could hear my mother screaming before I got to the door. They were in the living room, and he was pummeling her as she cowered and tried to escape. I launched myself at him like a missile, barreling into him with all my small might, trying to break it up. He picked me up without breaking stride and threw me across the room like a rag doll. I ran outside, and next thing I knew, there were lights and sirens. Miss Anne and other neighbors had heard the screaming, too, and called for help. I hid in the yard and watched. There were police cars and an ambulance. The police were talking to Dirty Harry outside. Neighbors were gathering in the street. Miss Anne clutched little Leon. I watched a stretcher being loaded into the ambulance.

That was the last time I ever saw my mother.

Neighbors took us in that night, and after that, social services came and we were all split up. Miss Anne wanted to keep Leon. I didn't know what had happened or where we were being taken. The grown-ups all just went about their official business, handing me off from one place to the next. I was soon a different boy than I had been just days before, and I knew exactly when I changed: in that moment when my father hurled me against the wall, and I felt the impact as much inside as I did outside, solid as pain. Shutting down, and shutting people out, made me feel safe, like a deadbolt sliding into place.

MY FIRST STOP IN THE FOSTER-CARE SYSTEM was with a couple who gave me a room by myself—the first I'd ever had—and enrolled me in a new school. They were kind to me, and their house was peaceful and quiet. I liked them and wanted to stay, and they wanted to keep me, but a week later, the lady from social services turned up again and said I couldn't live there anymore. No one said why. People back then thought you should protect children from the truth if it was sad or ugly, as if silence were a shelter. I would beat against its walls with my questions: What happened to my mother and father? Where were my brothers and sisters? I had promised to take care of them. Why couldn't we go home?

"Where's my mother?" I wailed when social services delivered me to a group home. I cried like there was no tomorrow.

"Your mother's gone," is all the foster-care people would tell me.

"I want my brothers! I want to be with my brothers!"

Someone took me in a room, sat me down, and took all my hair off. I had a big Afro, just like the cool older kids were wearing then. I may have been pint-sized, but my hair gave me swagger. I fought and screamed as they shaved my head and clouds of dark hair floated to the floor. I hated that. I hated the way I looked, the way they wanted me to be. I was lonely and frustrated and angry. As soon as the door opened, I bolted, and took off running. They caught me right away, wanted to know where I thought I was going.

"I'm just trying to find my brothers. Where are they?"

"We don't know where they're at."

I wasn't a troublemaker then. Not yet. I wasn't stealing or robbing or getting into fights. But in the group home, I was in a dorm room with a bunch of other kids, and they had their own reasons for being angry, and most of them were bigger and tougher than I was. You had to learn fast how to fight in a place like that. Especially if you looked like me, with light skin and a slight build. The other boys started right in with the taunts: "You can't fight, you a punk!" "You a pretty boy!"

I'll tell it to you straight, without any political correctness bullshit: Back when you had slaves, people used to say there were three kinds—field nigger, backyard nigger, and house nigger. What you were depended on your skin coloring. The darkest-skinned slaves worked the fields, then one notch up from that were the yard workers. But the slaves with the fairest skin, closest to white, they were the favored ones and given the jobs inside the master's house. They bowed and scraped for his leftovers. In modern times, being called a house nigger is about the worst insult one African American can hurl at another; it's saying you're beneath contempt, that you're nothing but a toady who thinks you're better than everybody else. In the group home, I was considered the house nigger. The half-breed who thought he was black but looked white. I got good enough at throwing a punch that the other kids left me alone. I was still miserable. We had to clean the toilets, mop the floors, and do a whole raft of chores. You couldn't get milk and cookies at night, or take a shower when you felt like it, or watch cartoons on a Saturday morning. I started smoking cigarettes. I kept running away. Sometimes I could manage to stay out a day or two until they found me. I'd beg food from a restaurant, and sometimes they'd give me something, sometimes not. I learned how to snatch an apple off a fruit stand, or a banana, and keep moving. Social services kept putting me in different group homes. One of them forced me to wear a diaper, figuring wrongly that I would be too humiliated to make a run for it. I was sent to some type of meeting to get counseling for anger.

"Why are you mad?" the group leader wanted to know.

"What do you think I'm mad about? Where's my family?"

SOMEONE FINALLY TOLD ME that my mother was dead, and I came to understand that my father had murdered her and the child she was carrying. I assumed Dirty Harry was in jail. But if there was a funeral for my mother, no one told me or took me, and if she had any people out there in the world, they never came for me. No matter. I didn't need anyone anymore. That only led to disappointment. That was the way it had always played out for me so far.

When I was around eleven, social services packed me up from the latest group home and drove me to the Bronx, where a foster family by the name of Coleman was going to take me in. I went inside the apartment and got the surprise of my life: all four of my younger brothers were there, too. We were finally going to get to live together again. I was happier than I had ever been. We were going to be part of a real family, stay in one school for a whole grade or longer, live an ordinary life like other kids. It's funny now to think how we had been through so much, but just fell back in together without pause, never stopping to fill in the blank of two missing years. Had my younger brothers been together all that time? Were they treated all right? Had Leon been with Miss Anne? I didn't ask then, and it's too late now. We just went on.

The Colemans—Ma and Pops now—already had a son of their own, Maurice, called Geese, who was around five or six at the time but still clung to his mother like a toddler. Mrs. Coleman was very laid-back, in her thirties, and heavyset. She was probably pretty as hell when she was younger and slimmer, you could tell by her face.

She was a housewife. They must have taken in foster kids before, because Mrs. Coleman didn't seem all that anxious about adding five rowdy boys to the household. Mr. Coleman worked as a security guard and came home every night. The two of them spoiled Geese rotten, and it became clear soon enough that we weren't going to be one big family so much as two separate ones, with my brothers and me as the less-worthy branch. The Colemans moved from the apartment in the Bronx to a duplex in St. Albans, Queens, where we could all fit. There was an upstairs apartment and a downstairs one. My brothers and I were put upstairs, and the Colemans locked the door to the main house downstairs at night. Mrs. Coleman also shooed us out if we didn't keep quiet while she was watching her favorite soap opera, *One Life to Live*.

Of my brothers, I was closest to Albert, who went by Al, and was two years younger than I was. Ernie was in between us, but Ernie was the loner of the bunch, content to sit by himself practicing his guitar all the time. Ernie wasn't into sports the way Al and I were, but he could swim like a shark, slicing through the water fast and neat, able to stay below the surface for the entire length of the public pool without coming up for air once. I called him Submariner. Ernie had stamina, and he was no coward. He was the first one of my family to fight me back and damn near whipped my butt. And it was probably Ernie who decided to put an end to my bullying by having all four brothers jump me once after I threw them out of my room. Ernie even came with his own canine backup unit: an insanely devoted brown-and-white mutt he had adopted named Rocky. Rocky always had Ernie's back and would attack even Ma or Pops if they didn't show Ernie the respect Rocky thought he deserved. If that dog thought I was coming for Ernie, I'd be on my ass. He bit my leg once when I was just arguing with my brother. "I'm gonna kill that dog," I threatened. Ernie just laughed. "No, you ain't." He knew Rocky would get me first.

Al lived for baseball and basketball, just like me, and was most likely to do reckless shit with me, like ride a bike down Bear Mountain straight into the lake. Al and I shared one of the two bedrooms in the upstairs apartment at the Colemans', and Michael, Ernie, and Leon bunked in the other one. Michael was the middle brother, the short one, as hardheaded as I was. He was not going to take any crap, and you'd best not offer him any. He loved martial arts and was always kicking or chopping the air or, if you made him mad, any vulnerable body part within striking distance. He could also do backflips and front flips. Finally, there was Leon, the baby. Leon was a follower. Leon wanted to be like me, but he was too sensitive to grow that tough a skin, and there was always a sweetness to him even after he followed in my footsteps to become a boxer. He was left-handed, so we called him Lefthand.

The house in St. Albans was near 208th and Murdock. We thought of it as a famous neighborhood. A popular radio host named Ed Lover was from there, plus Russell Simmons and Run DMC. We lived five blocks from LL Cool J. There was also a dude named Sundance who could've made the NBA but got screwed up on drugs. It was a nice, middle-class neighborhood, I guess you'd say. There was a little grocery store run by Mr. Dobbins and his son. Mr. Dobbins was fair, and if you stole from him, you had to be a real lowlife. You'd go in, get your candy or soda, and keep moving. He didn't give you the stink eye or tell you to get out like other storekeepers might when they saw a bunch of young neighborhood boys spill through the door. You'd hear of someone getting murdered a few blocks over on Jamaica Avenue or Linden

Boulevard. That wasn't our neighborhood. You'd hear of someone getting their ass whupped on Murdock, sure—we'd challenge people from other blocks to baseball, basketball, or football games, and every now and then we'd have our fights. But 208th and Murdock was safe.

Murdock had a dude named William as our private security patrol. Everyone knew you didn't mess with William or his two younger brothers, that you didn't come into our neighborhood with that bull jive. William was in his twenties. I don't know what all he was into, except I'll say that William did what he had to, to survive. When a drunk driver plowed into a house down the street and killed the little boy and girl playing out front, William flew out of his house three doors down and tackled the fleeing driver, pinning him until the cops arrived. I remember the loud bang of that crash, the smoking car sticking out of the wall, and the hysterical mother screaming for her babies. I could see body parts on the lawn. The image was like a horror show that flashes to this day across my mind. The neighbors hollered for William to get the driver. He was lucky William let him go to jail instead of to the morgue.

My own street-fighting skills were a work in progress. When I first moved in with the Colemans, the school I went to was in a Spanish neighborhood of the Bronx, and right off the bat, some older boys jumped me for my coat. They asked if I was in a gang—there were the Savage Skulls, the Savage Nomads, and a large assortment of other Savages all claiming their piece of turf. I wasn't about to just hand over my coat, so I fought, even though I was outnumbered three to one. They took my coat. But word got back that I'd fight, and after a while, the Spanish kids left me alone. I had a temper as a kid. I *hated* losing. Couldn't stand it. In sports, losing a game of basketball or baseball would send me over the edge, and God save the teammate who missed a winning shot or dropped a home-run ball. Eventually, boxing would change that, because if I lost, there was nobody to blame but me. But at twelve, I didn't have that passion or discipline yet—all I had was my anger, and there was plenty of it to go around. To my new classmates, I looked Spanish, but I wasn't Spanish, which left me open for the same half-breed ridicule I got from blacks. I didn't automatically belong anywhere and was always forced to prove myself. Whatever conflicts I found or got myself into inevitably trickled down to my brothers. I took them aside to tell them how it was going to be: "Look, any one of us gets in a fight, all of us jump 'em. You gotta just learn how to fight." Biting, kicking, scratching, whatever it took to win. I didn't stop until I saw blood. I never picked up a pipe or bat or anything to throw or hit a dude with, though. Everything was fair and square back then.

One day, this bully named Floyd came up and said he wanted to fight me. We went outside, and he bent over pretending he was tying his shoe. I knew he was going to come up swinging. He busted my nose. I busted his nose. He gave me a black eye. I gave him an ear scrape. The teachers broke us up.

"I'll see you tomorrow," said Floyd.

"See you tomorrow," I agreed.

We fought for several days like that until we called a truce and became friends. Same thing happened with my friend Arnie. It took a week of busted lips, torn clothes, and bloody noses before we became the best of friends. It was starting to dawn on me that any respect I got seemed to come through my fists. Fighting established who I was, what I would take and what I wouldn't, who I would stand up for and who I would put down. When I was in the eighth grade, a tangled romance involving Arnie's sister Marbles led me to cockily spread the word that I was going to fight their older brother, Donald, who happened to be the head of the Savage Skulls. Marbles called the gangbangers off, but one of the biggest and baddest dudes in the neighborhood delivered a message: "You got a lotta heart," he said, "a lotta heart." I know now how right he was, that fighting was slowly but surely giving me what a father should have—confidence, character, courage. Everybody else could abandon me, but I would never abandon myself.

At the Colemans', I never really felt like a son so much as a boarder. In the seven years I lived there, I never heard the words *I love you*. Pops would come home from work and settle into his basement domain for the evening. He had this big bucket he would fill with a block of ice, which he would then chip away at with a knife, creating a cold nest for his Seven Crown whiskey. He would sit there and watch baseball on the TV for hours, but he never once came to watch me play when I was in Little League or basketball. The trophies I won were lined up on top of the TV cabinet without any comment or even passing interest. We were both rabid Mets fans, but the shared interest never grew into anything resembling an actual bond. When the Mets were in the World Series one year, I ditched school, snuck back into the house knowing Ma would be gone that afternoon, and settled in to watch the daytime game on TV. Pops was no dummy, and he knew I would be there, and I knew he'd come home early and lay into me with his belt. But I made a calculated decision: it was worth the ass-whipping. Pops delivered, but so did the Mets. They won the game, and I considered the burning red welts on my backside to be the ticket price. If it had been Geese caught playing hooky to watch a ball game, the Colemans probably would have popped his pampered ass some popcorn and asked if he needed a bigger TV. When Geese said, "Ma, I want a bass guitar," he got it, boom, just like that. "Ma, I want a moped," boom, here you go. I asked for a five-dollar pair of Bruce Lee kung fu shoes and had to beg two days; Maurice got them instantly. I'd beg and beg and beg for hours for some little thing; Ma would look at me with disgust and say no. I got my first bike by stealing it. I was scared as heck. I saw a kid go into a store and leave his ten-speed unlocked outside. It looked fast, that bike, and I wanted it in the worst way. I made my choice in a matter of seconds and ran up, jumped on, and pedaled off, thinking all the time, *I can't get caught, I can't get caught, can't fall.* Back home, the Colemans immediately confronted me.

"Where'd you get that bike?"

"A friend gave it to me."

"What kind of friend give you that kind of bike?" They knew the story made no sense and had to suspect what had really happened, but they let it go. After that, stealing bikes became a thrilling hobby of sorts. First I would make some bull-jive bike out of extra parts I saved—no seat, tires torn up. Then I would leave that bike in place of whatever better bike I was stealing. I never did it in my own neighborhood.

Bikes weren't the only thing I helped myself to. Sometimes I would snatch a piece of fruit from a produce stand or go into a store and sneak a package of ham or baloney from the deli aisle and slip it into my pocket. My stomach was growling with hunger more often than not, it seemed. The Colemans locked their refrigerator to keep my brothers and me from getting an extra snack or glass of milk. "We already fed you" was the standard response if we came downstairs hungry at night or on a weekend afternoon. Maurice could have whatever he wanted whenever he wanted. I can remember angrily accusing the Colemans more than once of not loving us, not even caring for us, and just wanting the monthly check from child services. I don't remember either Ma or Pops ever telling me I was wrong about that.

Whatever money the state sent to support us, it sure didn't go toward clothes, because "the Dewey boys," as we came to be known in the neighborhood, were the clown fashion show of Murdock Avenue. Mrs. Coleman did the shopping and dressed us in cheap getups like Michael Jackson pants with stripes down the side, and red, white, and blue Skips tennis shoes. I hated how I looked. I yearned for a pair of black suede Converse 69 sneakers so bad, I took a paper route and got up at three in the morning to deliver the *New York Daily News* to fifty houses. I loaded most of the papers into a crate I had jerry-rigged onto the front of my bicycle and put the rest in a backpack, wobbling through St. Albans like an urban pack mule. At first, it would take me two trips, but it didn't take long for my legs to get so strong and lean, I could deliver all my papers making one loop without missing a breath. I'd finish up just before school. Earning my own paycheck gave me my first taste of what it was like to actually make choices about my life, small as they were. I could have a bag of chips when my stomach was growling, or lace up a pair of shoes that wouldn't get me laughed off the basketball court. I didn't ever want to be without my own money again. Money gave me freedom. Money let me belong to me, plain and simple.

Once I started at Andrew Jackson High School, though, I became too hip for a lowly paper route. I quit my job. I even stopped playing baseball. I thought I was all grown up, with better things to do. I had my priorities, and tenth grade is exactly when they all started going backward. My best buddy, Herbie, was going to a different high school—one for troubled kids in Manhattan—but we hung out together at a park on Hollis Avenue, playing basketball. We were good. I was a mean jumper, and Herbie could come in underneath and steal a ball before the other guy realized he was there. When we weren't shooting hoops at the park, we were hanging out smoking Newports and reefer and drinking Old English 800 beer from a place across the street. The old-timers in their twenties and thirties hanging out in front of the beer store or chilling in the park would help us out, buy our quarts for us.

"Aight, I ain't got nothing to do with you, you get caught," they'd warn.

"Aight," we'd agree.

Pops was the likeliest one to catch me when I brought the party home to our place, but I knew he would stay put in his basement hideout drinking his own bottle as long as we kept quiet. Pops was crazy, but he was fair. We'd be in and out till two or three in the morning. When it got too rowdy, Pops would charge up the stairs, bellowing as he came. "Goddammit, stop making all that noise!" Dudes would be jumping out the window and up on the roof to get away. The Colemans never seemed to have a clue about all the wasted teenagers up there. I got so high on one Friday night that I passed out in my clothes, slept right through Saturday, and didn't wake up until Sunday. No one even checked to see if I was okay. I think Pops tried in the beginning to get us to go in the right direction by punishing us when we acted up, like grounding us with no TV, or giving us the belt, but once he lost control of me, he lost control of all of us. I may have been the first to turn rebellious, but my brothers closed the gap quick enough. We were all stealing stuff, except Leon. He'd try to follow behind me but I'd push him away.

THERE WAS THIS OLDER WHITE GUY NAMED RALPH who drove a big white truck and would buy any damn thing we brought him.

"Hey, Ralph, I got a lawnmower," I would say.

"Looks like a real piece of shit."

"What'll you give me for it?"

"Five dollars."

We'd go into garages and steal tools. There was also good money taking copper off houses—the waterpipes, mainly—and selling it to junkyards.

It was during my teens that two of my lost older siblings briefly appeared, each showing up for a quick, awkward visit arranged by social services. My sister, Janice, offered a stunning piece of news.

"Dewey, you know I seen Pop," she said, meaning Dirty Harry.

I had locked our father out of my memory and thrown away the key, secure in my belief that he was rotting away in prison somewhere.

"What do you mean?" I asked Janice now. She told me she had caught sight of him out on the street one day.

"I remember those glasses," she said. "He didn't come up, didn't approach me, but I seen him."

We left it there, neither of us wanting to discuss it more. We didn't, in fact, have much of anything to say to each other. We'd been separated and had lived our separate lives. What we had left in common was something too ugly, too painful, for either of us to want to revisit. Janice got up and said good-bye. I never saw her again.

My brother Tony's visit was less unsettling but still awkward. I'd never even met Tony before. He was seven years older than I was, a grown man when we first laid eyes on each other. He was one of the "new" siblings my mother had told me were going to come live with us just before Dirty Harry gave her that last beating. Tony was a decent guy, but we were polar opposites. Tony didn't have the dangerous polish that street life gives you, that cold steel, urban gleam. He was country. His language, his demeanor, his clothing all told the story of a world less complicated than mine. You could tell he was a worrier. He came to see me at the Colemans' a couple of times, and even though we were only in the beginner stage of getting to know each other as brothers, he stepped up later when I needed a refuge away from New York City.

As maddening and heartless as it seemed, the bureaucracy that ran my childhood did make an effort to give my younger brothers and me a little taste of the good life every now and then. We were taken on orphan-kid outings to Yankee Stadium and Shea Stadium. We got to go to an Al Green concert. There would be field trips to cultural events around the city, and different educational or vocational training programs they offered us. I blew most of those off, too young and cocky to recognize opportunity when it tapped me on the shoulder. The one privilege I did take advantage of to its fullest was the annual summer vacation for foster kids at Camp Comanche. It was a sleep-away camp on a pretty little lake, which I loved to dive into and swim all the way across, powering through the cool water like my man with the seven Olympic gold medals around his neck, Mark Spitz. Mark Spitz had it all: the athleticism, the swooning women, the hero poster, the Ferrari. Pushing your body to the limit like that, reaching peak performance, was something I really admired.

At school, I was a good student when I bothered to do the work, which wasn't all that often. I could sort of skate by in some courses, like math, which I loved and was pretty good at; I liked to sit down and figure out the problems. Math was straightforward: a math problem told you whether you had solved it or not, and the right answer could always be proven. I enjoyed science, too. Science made me think and see things differently, appreciate that things weren't always what they seemed. If I had stuck with it, I probably would have been a natural at physics—I was an ongoing experiment in energy, force, and motion, with the scars to prove it. English was another story. English was my downfall. I would write everything in street language, and my papers would come back all smashed up. Hyper as I'd always been, it was hard for me to sit still all day long in some classroom, and by my freshman year, school was rapidly losing its hold on me. Even the lure of extracurricular sports wasn't enough. I'd been told I had real talent on the baseball field, for example, but I didn't try out for my high school team. It felt like I was outgrowing everything good in my life, like Camp Comanche, and I couldn't go back. I stopped playing hoops and started skipping school to spend more time on what I now considered my regular activities—getting high, hanging out, and stealing.

The first time I robbed someone, I did it just because I wanted to be accepted by the older kids who recruited me to be their lookout. They were mugging people, just running up and taking their money. You didn't need a weapon; nobody but a fool would demand proof that the bulge in your hoodie pocket was a gun or knife and not your fist. We stayed out of our own neighborhood, and we never robbed a woman—snatching pocketbooks was against our code. I was scared as hell that first time. From what I can remember, we got seven or eight dollars, then rode our bikes fast as we could out of there. We used the money to go get high. I never could rob anybody unless I was high. I'd try to do it normal, then I'd back off it. But you get high, you get bold, and it's *to hell with it,* and there you are, stealing.

AT SIXTEEN, I DROPPED OUT OF HIGH SCHOOL. I don't know if it was coun-selors, social services, or the Colemans, but someone gave me an-other chance, with a spot in an alternative school. I didn't last even two weeks. I had made my choice about the life I wanted, and I wanted my freedom. The Colemans probably should have just kicked me out, but they didn't, and I would come and go from the upstairs apartment with my brothers as I pleased, sometimes disappearing for weeks at a time. The apartment was a shambles by then—nothing had ever been maintained or repaired or even really cleaned, with five wild boys living in it. There were holes in the wall, broken-down beds; it was trashed. Downstairs where the family lived, it was middle class, but up where we were kept, it was ghetto. The Colemans didn't give a shit, and we didn't, either.

My first serious brush with the law happened in my teens when I spotted some guy walking along with his stereo box. He looked like a pussy, so I decided to rob him. I stuck my finger in a potato chip bag, told him it was a gun, and walked away with the stereo. Police caught me fifteen minutes later up on Hollis Avenue, where I planned on selling it. I was sauntering up the street with this just-stolen stereo, playing it loud. That's how high and brazen I was. The cops took me up to the 105th Precinct, then to Central Booking. From there, it was off to Rikers Island and my first time behind bars. It was scary. Rikers was a zoo. A very dangerous human zoo. Right away, my prized black suede Converse 69ers were stolen.

I yelled out into the cellblock, "Listen, whoever got my sneak-ers, give me a fair fight!"

A friendly informant pointed out the thief, and I made plans for a counterattack with what was known as a lock-sock. You could get a lock from the canteen to safeguard your clothes and hygiene items. If you stuffed it into a sock—I planned to add a couple of bars of soap for good measure—you could swing it at someone's head and bust a nose or even crack a skull. Hit the kneecap hard enough, and you could make a guy buckle. My sneaker revenge was supposed to go down when we were let out for rec, but the guards saw what was about to happen and pulled us apart. The other inmate had a pen. At Sing Sing, I would learn that there's a way you can turn a simple ballpoint pen into a deadly weapon. Convict 101.

I ended up in juvenile detention for sixteen months for that robbery, but once I was out, it was back to business as usual.

One of my favorite ways to kill time as a dropout was to take the subway into Manhattan and spend all day in Times Square. This was when it was a neon jungle of peep shows, dives, and street hustlers. There was a big multiplex movie theater, and I would either buy a ticket if I had the money or sneak in, then spend the entire day watching kung fu and other martial arts films, slipping from one theater to the next. I'd emerge only when I got hungry, around four or five in the afternoon, blinded by the sunlight. If I didn't have any money on me to buy a hamburger or slice of pizza, I'd look for someone to rob for some quick, easy cash. Gambling spots were an easy target. You knew people had money and could see who was walking away with what. I liked to shoot dice myself, and I could make a hundred, two hundred dollars playing craps in the park. Then I'd go down to Delancey Street, buy fifty pair of underwear, and resell them for quadruple what I'd paid. I liked to run the craps games myself. I could start with a quarter and leave with three hundred dollars at the end of a good day. I used brand-new dice, and I always made sure my dice were legit. I was a kid playing grown-ass men who were thirty, forty, fifty years old. You don't come in with no damned loaded dice. You wanna die, that's the quickest way: mess with someone's money. I was likable. I'd give a store fifty bucks and get beer on tab. I had people trusting me. When I owed, I paid. So my reputation was good. Every now and then, if a guy was arrogant and I didn't like him, I would go rob him. And I still hadn't lost my childish temper about being a sore loser: if you won money off me, chances were good that I would come get it back. The kind of people I targeted weren't the kind who were likely to report it. The streets had their own Darwinian law, and when it came to survival, I had been fit since I was six and my father was throwing me against walls.

BACK AT 208TH AND MURDOCK, I got into a fight one day with a boy around my age named Stanley Jackson. I don't even remember what it was about, but I got the best of him, right there in the middle of the street. Word got around. The old guy who ran the store looked at me and said knowingly, "Oh, you the guy who beat up on Stanley." Stanley had two black eyes and a busted lip. I was good with nothing but a couple of scrapes. "Yeah," I told the storekeeper, "that was me."

Stanley was no punk. He was a stickup guy who hung out with a Rastafarian named Barney. Not long after the beat-down, Stanley and Barney rode past me on a bike, and Barney pointed a rifle at me. I looked at him, looked at the rifle, and wondered for a heartbeat if I was about to be gunned down. Stanley and Barney just drove past and kept going.

The following night, there was a dance party at Andrew Jackson High School. I was somewhere else, out doing my thing, but my brother Ernie, the music-loving guitar player, went to the dance. When he came out, Barney and Stanley were waiting for him. Stanley jumped him and stabbed Ernie through the heart with a butcher knife. I came home that night, and the whole house was quiet and still. Pops was in his usual chair in the basement. He told me my brother had been murdered, then picked up his knife and stabbed his block of ice.

"Dewey, I know if you was there, that would never have happened," he said. He was crying.

It was the first time in all those years that he had shown any goddamn love for me and my brothers, and it took death for him to do it.

Everyone who knew me thought I was going to kill Stanley Jackson, given the chance.

I knew it, too.

Murder had redefined me again.

3

WHEN I LOST ERNIE, I LOST MORE OF MYSELF. You can make yourself a stone, but life can still chisel away at you, and this blow splintered me into too many sharp pieces to sweep up and put together again. Ernie's death made me realize how much I loved my younger brothers, and what lengths I would go to in order to keep that childhood promise I had made to my mother to always take care of them. Stanley Jackson had been sentenced to juvenile detention for Ernie's murder and would be out in sixteen months. Once he was free, he would be lucky to live sixteen minutes. I had every intention of avenging my brother's death. I wouldn't need any knife or a gun, and I wouldn't be sneaking up behind Stanley either. He could look me in the eye while he died like the coward he was. They could lock me up for the rest of my life, and I would consider it a fair price to pay. I was hurting so bad, I couldn't even think straight. Nothing felt right anymore.

I stopped hanging out with my friends and just kept to myself, letting the streets wash over me and swallow me up like the tide. I would disappear from the Colemans' for days or even a week or two at a time. I didn't want to stay still anywhere for long and would sleep out on the streets even when I knew I had a warm bed to go home to. I'd hole up in abandoned buildings along with the junkies and winos and crazies. When I got too scared or lonely for that life, I would find a woman with a place of her own and the need of some company; I always looked and carried myself older than I was, and most of the women I picked up in bars had no idea I was only a teenager. Nobody could tell me what to do anymore, and the Colemans didn't even pretend. As far as I was concerned, the streets treated me better than my supposed family did: If I was hungry, I didn't have to wait for someone to give me permission to eat and say how much I could have. If I wanted nice clothes, I could buy them myself. I loved the feeling of going out without a dime in my pocket and having four or five hundred dollars by the next afternoon, just by sitting on my ass shooting dice. Larceny was my backup career, and I was damned good at that, too. If a guy was walking down the street in the garment district with hundreds of dresses and he turned his back, I could steal a whole rack before he knew it. When you're bold and you act like it's yours, you're good. Every now and then, I'd go to a museum or art gallery where they have those jars sitting out for donations. I'd throw my coat over the jar and walk out with it. It's not as easy as it sounds when your brain is telling your face to look casual and your feet to run like hell. Guess it's a good thing my taste still ran to martial arts posters, or I might have passed up the donation jar and graduated to art thief, instead. Stealing made me feel superior: I didn't need to work some crap job at McDonald's six days a week for a puny paycheck like the other high school dropouts; I was clever enough to rake in a lot more cash, pay no taxes, and keep my own hours. If someone was stupid enough to leave a jar full of cash out in the open, or go strutting down Hollis Avenue with a brand-new boom box, well then, they got what was coming. And what was coming was me. Dewey Bozella, career criminal in the making.

Where I drew the line was dealing drugs. That game is kill or be killed. You gotta be too cold-blooded, and I knew I didn't have that in me. Some dude comes up to you begging—*I need it, I need it, I need it*—you have to kick his ass across the street. Some broken-down woman comes up offering to do you for drugs, you have to push her away. You have to be suspicious 24/7, even with your supposed friends. You don't know who to trust, who's going to snitch on you. I knew that sooner or later, you had to kill somebody to make an example. That wasn't me, and even in my worst times, I held myself apart from that whole ugly scene.

I wasn't happy with my life, but I can't say I was deeply troubled by it at that age either. Breaking away from the streets is harder than it probably sounds to people who've never been there: the ones who ask why the juvenile delinquent didn't just choose to stay in school, or why the battered wife didn't just choose to leave, or why the panhandler on the subway didn't just get a job. Your mind-set can follow you no matter how far you run. When I was around seventeen, I remember I decided to go to Washington, D.C., for no particular reason at all. I bought a ticket, boarded a bus, and was looking at the Capitol dome a few hours later. I ended up staying in D.C. for a week, just living on the streets same as I did in New York, not even pretending to go see the sights or be a different type of person. Then I got on a bus and headed back north. I didn't have any plans for my future—not even a rough sketch, let alone a blueprint—and I assumed that tomorrow would always look just like today. I couldn't have cared less. People use that term all the time, but after burying Ernie, it became my reality. It would have been impossible for me to care less about anything and everything else.

AFTER ABOUT THREE OR FOUR MONTHS OF BUMPING ALONG LIKE THIS, my older brother, Tony, approached me again. Tony had seen plenty of at-risk kids like me in his counseling job with the Division of Youth, and he knew someone had to care enough to grab them by the scruff and jerk them back to keep them from going over the edge. With no one else willing to fill the role in my life, he volunteered for the part. He knew that he had to get me out of the city if I was going to have any chance at all to turn my life around.

"Hey, man, why don't you just come upstate and live with me?" Tony suggested.

Beacon was no Mayberry—it had its own problems, and they were getting worse by the day—but its ugly side was nothing compared to New York City's. The idea grew on me, and I agreed to relocate.

The ride up the Hudson River was only an hour or so by train, but it was distant enough to feel like a fresh start. And maybe I would stop dwelling on Ernie's death if I weren't living in the same house he had lived in, walking the same streets he had walked, seeing the same people from the neighborhood he had known. Tony thought I could find a job, maybe learn a trade, get my GED. I admit I was slow to follow through, though. Twenty miles to the north, Poughkeepsie had a more urban feel than sleepy Beacon, and there was a bus that dropped me off right by Mansion Square Park, where the town troublemakers and lowlifes hung out. It was a whole lot easier to cling to my old slickster ways than it was to focus on straightening up the small mess I'd already made of my life. I didn't make any real friends—the homies didn't like my light skin or my big-city attitude—but if nothing else, I at least felt I was in my element. Just how badly I misread their animosity, and just how alone I truly was, didn't become clear until I was sitting trial for murder.

MY ARREST IN THE CRAPSER SLAYING IN 1977 WAS ALL OVER TV AND THE PAPERS— the case had been front-page news—and to this day, I don't know whether it was the publicity that made Tony nervous or whether my brother actually doubted my innocence. If my own flesh and blood thought I was the kind of monster who could do something like that to someone's grandmother, then I didn't want to know, and I didn't ask when he kicked me to the curb after I was released without charge. It was no big deal: I was used to disappointing people and having them disappoint me. A woman I'd been seeing named Viola was more than happy to take me right in. Viola was thirty-five and had three kids. Her husband had been abusive and got sent away after he shot her in the stomach. I met Viola through her brother, and we just hit it off. Flirting with older women was such a natural reflex for me, I was more surprised when I didn't score than when I did. One time, I picked up a clerk working behind the desk when I went to file for unemployment. When it came to the part where you're supposed to list your skills and say what kind of job you're looking for, I turned on the charm.

"I'm going to tell you, I'm straight street," I boasted, then asked her out for a cup of coffee.

"You got a lotta nerve for your little ass," she shot back.

We ended up kicking it for a while, then I moved on.

Coming up through the foster-care system taught me how to handle myself around social services if nothing else, and I was a smooth operator when it came to manipulating the system. I could walk inside, drop my voice low and dejected, say "I'm living on the streets and things are not going well," and walk back out with $315 for a room and $100 in food stamps. Same drill with collecting unemployment checks: I just filled out the paperwork and waited for it to kick in. It was all the same untended donation jar to me. Accountability was a joke, and I laughed all the way to Mansion Square Park where I spent shiftless hours gambling and smoking reefer. The difference was that now I had a big fat target on my back. As far as the Poughkeepsie cops were concerned, I was a killer who had gotten away with murdering a defenseless old lady. They made a point of hassling me at every turn. They arrested me for peeing in public twice on the same day. Another time, I was fixing a bicycle and had a screwdriver and pair of pliers in my pocket. Police rolled by me, jumped out, and told me to get up against the wall. "You're under arrest for burglary," I was told that time. The harassment was blatant and irritating, but if the purpose was to run me out of town, it wasn't working. Over and over we'd go through the same drill: they'd cuff me, book me, then release me when they didn't have enough to charge me. Not that I was always innocent. Or smart. I once got into a scuffle with a guy who turned out to be an undercover cop. Then there was the shopkeeper on the pedestrian Main Mall in downtown Poughkeepsie who ordered me to "get outta my store, you nigger" and got his front window kicked in as a result.

In the early 1980s, Poughkeepsie was on the downslide, like a pretty young heiress gone to rot. Look it up in the history books, and you'll see that it was once considered the "Queen City of the Hudson River," where rich New York families like the Vanderbilts and Astors built their weekend mansions. There were famous factories, like IBM, Smith Brothers cough drops, and the printing company that made Little Golden Books for kids. Poughkeepsie was also home to Vassar College for Ivy League women. The downtown area was known for its fancy soda fountains and fine shops, and up until the end of World War II, the waterfront was thriving with industry. But when suburbs started becoming popular in the 1950s, Poughkeepsie began to lose its shine. The downtown shops couldn't compete with the malls outside of town where there was plenty of free parking, and the federal money that poured in for "urban renewal" ended up creating crime-riddled projects. When the laws changed about keeping mental patients locked up, the Main Mall that was supposed to revive downtown became a magnet instead for the now-homeless crazy people who'd been released from the state hospital in town. Crime was increasing, and so were racial tensions. People—mostly white—were fleeing the city at a record pace. In 1950, you would have found around forty-one thousand folks living in Poughkeepsie; by 1980, there weren't even thirty thousand. There were still some old mansions down by the riverfront, but they were crumbling and boarded up, the ballrooms taken over by squatters and crackheads. Downtown was considered dangerous. In the neighborhoods surrounding places like Mansion Square Park, there was an uneasy mix of white old-timers and minority newcomers. I still toggled back and forth between Manhattan and Poughkeepsie, and, despite the cold welcome, Dutchess County was starting to take root as my home base.

Not long after the Crapser case was dismissed, I got busted for robbery, pleaded guilty, and got locked up in state prison in Fishkill for two years. I hated prison, and the lifestyle that used to make me feel so cocky was wearing on me. Doing it when you were in your twenties was one thing, but I'd seen enough guys still hustling in their forties, their fifties, and even their sixties to know that wasn't where I wanted to end up. I came out of Fishkill determined to turn myself around once and for all, to make a serious attempt at going straight. I had grandiose dreams—childhood fantasies, really—of making it in Hollywood. I'd always wanted to be an actor and just felt like I had it in me. I admired the cool, sophisticated stars of my childhood, like Sidney Poitier, Bill Cosby in *I Spy,* and Roger Moore as James Bond. I loved the hell out of James Cagney and John Wayne and Jerry Lewis. My favorite actor was Steve McQueen in *Bullitt.* I used to try to imitate them all. I was the kid who would see *Spider-Man,* then go outside and try to climb a building. I didn't want to just watch a great performance, I wanted to be inside it. People always found that strange about me, how by myself I was. I even liked opera. I doubt there were any other dudes like me out there boosting stereos and then listening to Pavarotti. It was as if I had one self that belonged just to me, and the other one who lived on the outside. Changing my life meant learning how to finally give that inner self his say. In 1983, I decided to follow my heart as well as my impulses for once, and I set off for California intent on becoming a movie star. I'm not sure whether I was that naive, or that arrogant, but after a forgettable bus trip across the country and a few frustrating months in Los Angeles, I knew that I was East Coast through and through and got back on the bus heading the other way. The thing about Hollywood is if you ain't in, you ain't getting in. It takes connections. Even in modeling it takes money to make money. I didn't have the five hundred bucks I needed to get a portfolio done. So I lived in a fleabag room near the bus station and did what I knew: I went on welfare and spent hours gambling and shooting baskets in the park. My only brushes with fame were spotting some guy from the movie *Fame* and glimpsing Sylvester Stallone while I was working in a restaurant. I thought my chance had come for sure when I came across a film shoot on a downtown sidewalk one afternoon. The actor-director Tim Reid was shooting a scene where he was a homicide detective investigating a holdup at a liquor store. During a break in filming, I approached him, hoping to become an extra.

"Yo, Mr. Reid, what can I do, man?" I demanded brashly. "How do I get a part?"

"You got a hundred dollars?" he asked me. "First thing you need to do is get a portfolio. Professional headshot will cost you a hundred dollars."

He went back to work, and I went back to New York. End of that scene.

BACK IN NEW YORK, I ENROLLED IN DUTCHESS COUNTY COMMUNITY COLLEGE, aiming to get first my GED and then an associate's degree. I cobbled together a few part-time jobs to support myself—buffing floors in the predawn hours at the Rite-Aid, pounding nails and laying tiles at construction sites.

During my free time, I chased another dream. I began riding my bike out to New Paltz, where boxing great Floyd Patterson had turned an old barn on his chicken ranch into a gym for at-risk kids and aspiring young fighters. Patterson had been only twenty-one years old when he knocked out Archie Moore to become the youngest undisputed world heavyweight champion in history. He'd already won an Olympic gold medal at seventeen after being trained by the legendary Cus D'Amato at the old Gramercy Gym. He held the world title for five years, becoming the first to regain the crown after briefly losing it. He was humble even then. It was in defeat, he was often quoted as saying, that a man reveals himself. By the time our paths crossed, he had been retired from the ring for a good fifteen years and was intent on teaching street kids the discipline that boxing commands. Floyd's childhood was similar to my own. He was one of eleven kids, a chronic runaway and petty thief who had spent more time out on the streets than in the classroom. He'd gotten sent to reform school, where he was introduced to the sport he credited with saving his life. Now he was intent on giving other troubled young people the same ticket out of poverty and struggle. He and his wife had even adopted one of his most promising pupils; Tracy Patterson would eventually go on to become a world champ in the bantam and featherweight divisions.

Floyd noticed me hanging around the barn, watching him train Tracy and the others.

"Can you box?" he asked me one afternoon.

"I can fight a little bit," I said. I had usually come out on top in any street brawls I'd gotten into.

He put me in the ring to spar with Danny Chapman, the top-rated fighter in the club. When I caught Danny with a lucky punch, Floyd issued a quiet directive from the sidelines.

"Cut loose!"

Danny pummeled me with body shots and knocked the air clear out of me. When the bell rang, I got the hell out of there. Floyd called after me.

"Where you going?"

"I'll be back," I wheezed.

Floyd Patterson's experience overwhelmed me, but there was not one arrogant or egotistical bone in that man's rock-solid body. He was a very calm, mild-mannered person who commanded respect just by the way he carried himself. He didn't expect any payment for training us, and when I asked how much it cost to join his Huguenot Boxing Club, he thought about it for a minute before telling me it would be ten dollars a month. We both understood it was about the commitment, not the cash. I showed up every day, either bicycling or hitchhiking the ten country miles to get there. From the start, Floyd showed me how seriously I had to take the sport.

"You can't just go out there fighting," he lectured me. "You gotta go out there thinking."

Boxing is about strategy and endurance, not brute strength. You have to learn how to read your opponent, anticipate his moves, catch him off guard, wear him down. Most of all, you have to stay on your feet, try never to let them see you faltering. I thought the push-ups, weight training, and jumping jacks I'd always done had me in pretty good shape, but Floyd thought otherwise. He told me to work on my wind and my conditioning. When I got off work buffing the floors at Rite-Aid, I would set out running through the deserted streets of Poughkeepsie in combat boots. Even the cops got used to the sight of me and just waved or nodded as I jogged past at three or four in the morning. I'd do a few miles, go home, take a shower, get some rest, and do my calisthenics later on. Everything I did, I was working my way up the ladder, increasing my stamina. Sit-ups, push-ups, dips, mountain climbers, toe touches by the hundreds. Up to five hundred jumping jacks. Sometimes in Mansion Square Park, I'd spot Floyd Patterson on one of his own jogs. If he didn't want people to bother him, he'd put a newspaper over his head while he sat on a bench waiting to be picked up and taken home. I never approached him there. That was his time, his space, and I respected that.

In the Huguenot ring, Floyd would sometimes come out and spar with you himself to show you a point. He taught me how to work a jab. It doesn't get better than that, having a world champ step into the ring with you to show you how it's done. Patterson had been famous for keeping his gloves high, in front of his face, in what sportswriters used to call his "peekaboo stance." Then he'd just spring forward and catch his opponent with unexpected hooks. When he hung up his gloves for good, Patterson's professional record was 55-8-1 and forty knockouts. Some interviewer once commented that he might hold some record for being knocked down the most, and Floyd quickly jabbed back: "I also got up the most."

One time when I was hitting the bag, Floyd planted himself next to me.

"What're you doing?" he wanted to know.

"What do you mean? I'm hitting the bag!"

"No," he chastised me. "Don't just hit the bag. Pretend it's an opponent."

That was the essence of his approach: Always be on point. *Always.*

The club had some fighters on the ticket in the hinterlands of New Jersey one night, and Floyd invited me to come along to watch. We won three fights and lost one (that was on one of my sparring partners, who got too cocky for his own good). I was busy watching some of the other fights, and they forgot about me. I went outside and they were gone. I was in the middle of fucking nowhere and had no idea how I was going to hitch a ride all the way back to the Poughkeepsie projects. I was mulling this over in the parking lot when Floyd drove up.

"I knew I forgot somebody," he said by way of apology. Floyd never lost his cool. I never saw him mad, or even frustrated.

I couldn't be hurt or angry about being left behind—I was more amazed that Floyd had gotten a full half hour down the highway, halfway home, and had still bothered to turn back for me. In the coming years, his faltering memory and the onset of Alzheimer's disease would force him to resign as New York State's athletics commissioner. But he remembered me that night.

I never got the chance to tell him why I stopped showing up all of a sudden.

SIX YEARS AFTER I'D BEEN ARRESTED FOR THE CRAPSER MURDER—with insufficient evidence to bring charges—a former girlfriend caught wind of a new warrant out for the same case. When I heard, I was visiting an old New York City friend, Leon's mentor, Allen Thomas. I couldn't believe that this old case was coming back to haunt me now, just when everything in my life was going right. I called the Poughkeepsie police, pretending to be some detective working a case in New York City.

"You looking for Bozella?" I asked.

"Yeah, we got a warrant for murder out on him," came the answer.

I hung up, stunned but furious. I waited a few minutes and called back, identifying myself by name this time.

"Yo, you got a warrant out for me?" I demanded.

The cop on the other end said something about a misdemeanor, but I called his bluff.

"That's bullshit! I just called and they confirmed there's a murder warrant," I said. "I got nothing to hide. I'm coming up there tomorrow and turning myself in."

They picked me up and cuffed me while I was walking to the police station. I figured it would be a rerun of my 1977 arrest, and I'd be released soon enough. Prosecutors hadn't had any evidence to charge me the first time, and I knew there was no way that could have changed, since I'd never been inside Emma Crapser's apartment and had never laid a hand on her. I was dumbfounded when an indictment came down for second-degree murder. I pleaded "not guilty" at my arraignment and began reviewing the case with my court-appointed defense lawyer, Mickey Steiman, and his colleague, David Steinberg. Mickey was maybe a decade older than I was, with a 'fro to rival my own and a commitment to seeing justice served, though neither of us could have predicted it would be so sorely tested when he agreed to represent me. Mickey and David studied every document the prosecution turned over and conducted their own investigation. They felt confident that no jury would convict me. The entire case against me was built around the finger-pointing of two hard-core juvenile offenders whose testimony against me had come with get-out-of-jail-free deals so sweet even their own attorneys could scarcely believe it. The stories Wayne Moseley and Lamar Smith told were inconsistent and confusing at best, and flat-out contradictory at worst. Mickey thought it read like the script of a bad B movie with a cast full of shifty liars, thugs, and lowlifes. He was smelling a slam-dunk victory for us in the courtroom.

"There's not one piece of evidence tying you to this," he stressed.

The trial began on November 23, 1983, the day before Thanks-giving. The prosecutor, William O'Neill, was the same assistant district attorney for Dutchess County who had tried and failed to charge me for the crime as a teenager. His star witnesses were people I knew barely or not at all. Seven men and five women, none of them black, were selected as a jury of my peers. They learned the gruesome details about what had happened to Emma Crapser at the same time I did, as my trial unfolded.

Ms. Crapser lived alone in the ground-floor apartment of a small brick house at 15 North Hamilton Street in Poughkeepsie, in a neighborhood that had gotten rougher over the years as down-town Poughkeepsie started to die out. Her great-niece, Evelyn Pet-terson, sold ladies' undergarments in one of the small businesses still struggling to survive—The Shape Shop was visible from Emma's back stoop, and Evelyn checked on her elderly aunt every day. Ms. Crapser lived a quiet life, renting the upstairs apartment out to a couple to supplement her monthly Social Security check. Her four-room apartment was cluttered with stacks of old newspapers and magazines, and the tchotchkes of a long lifetime. There was a Goodyear Tire store on one side of her house, and another house converted to apartments on the other side. Some of the black teen-agers and young men seen going in and out of the neighboring house were said to belong to a group of Five Percenters. Five Per-centers were a breakaway faction of the Nation of Islam—younger guys mostly from the street, who believed that only five percent of the earth's inhabitants knew the truth and were capable of en-lightening the rest. The Five Percenters considered themselves God, and white people oppressors. Across the street from Ms. Crapser's house was a parking lot and an ambulance service. The garage door was open on the night of June 14, 1977.

Julia Emma Crapser was ninety-two years old, frail with poor hearing, but she was still sharp enough to know something wasn't quite right about the plumber who had shown up unexpectedly at her door earlier in the day and talked his way inside, saying he had been sent to check a leak that she knew nothing about, and he certainly hadn't reported to the service she regularly used. After he left, claiming he needed to get a stepladder and would be back later, the old woman called her plumbing company and discovered that they hadn't dispatched anyone. "I had another scare today," she told her niece, recounting the odd encounter with the man pretending to be a plumber. Ms. Crapser had been burglarized before, and she was worried. That evening, a couple picked her up for their usual Tuesday night bingo game at St. Joseph's Catholic Church. Emma Crapser won ten dollars. The friends dropped her off around eleven o'clock and the husband walked her to the front door. Ms. Crapser unlocked her apartment door, then turned back in the vestibule to wave good-bye.

Evelyn Petterson found the apartment door unlocked the next morning when she dropped by on the way to open her shop, and a quick glance inside told her the place had been ransacked. She could see her elderly aunt's favorite rocking chair tipped on its side. She backed out and called the police. Emma Crapser was dead on her kitchen floor. Her arms and legs were bound with telephone cords and the cord from her own hearing aid, and several pieces of cloth had been shoved into her mouth, including an eighty-eight-inch length of crocheted lace. What looked like a chisel was sticking out of her mouth—the killer had apparently used that to stuff all the cloth down her throat. A T-shirt and lady's slip were wrapped around her head and knotted. The coroner concluded that she had been suffocated to death, and also brutally beaten. Several ribs were broken, and there was damage to her liver, as well. She was still wearing her winter coat, and her watch had stopped at 10:58 P.M., leading investigators to believe that the killer or killers were already inside her apartment when she came home from bingo and interrupted a burglary. The upstairs neighbors had been home that evening and told police they hadn't seen or heard anything unusual.

The only time in my life I ever saw Emma Crapser was when the prosecutor brought out the crime-scene photos he had of her trussed, gagged, and battered body and slapped them on the table in front of me during the trial. Tears of disbelief and outrage filled my eyes.

"Man, I never done nothing like that!" I remember shouting. "I ain't do no shit like this. You got to be kidding me! You got the wrong man! You're outta your damn mind!"

Someone—I was too upset even to know whether it was the judge, the bailiff, or my own attorney—told me to calm down, and I swallowed back my tears and horror. What happened to that poor woman was barbaric, the work of a psychopath. That I was being falsely accused of doing it was an anguish I couldn't bear, like a public declaration that I was a vicious animal. Assistant District Attorney William O'Neill looked at me, with pure contempt in his eye. We would face each other in court time after time in the years to come, and he never once brought those pictures out again.

My name, it turned out, wasn't the first, second, or third that came up in connection with the Crapser murder. Right after the murder, police also interrogated a kid named Lamar Smith and his pals Wayne Moseley and Elbert "Sweet Pea" Pittman. They all had records, and a detective reported having spotted Smith, his brother, Stanley, Pittman, and an unidentified person near the Crapser residence about four hours before the murder. Police and prosecutor's records showed they all offered up alibis and denied knowing anything about the crime when they were first questioned. Four days after detectives interviewed him, though, Lamar was busted on a larceny charge and, with some prodding from his interrogators, changed his story about the night of Ms. Crapser's murder. Now he claimed that he had seen me and Wayne Moseley jimmying the front door of 15 North Hamilton that night while Pittman served as lookout. Moseley and his mother both swore before the grand jury that Wayne, then fifteen, was home that night watching TV on his mother's bed. That was when the grand jury decided there wasn't enough evidence to return an indictment against me—or anyone else.

Fast-forward to 1983. Wayne Moseley and Lamar Smith were both in prison on felony convictions. Detectives paid Wayne and Lamar a visit and offered them sweetheart deals to get out of jail immediately with blanket immunity from prosecution if they cooperated in the still-unsolved Crapser murder—specifically, my suspected role in it. Lamar Smith changed his story: he claimed I had talked about wanting to boost a stereo while hanging out in Mansion Square Park earlier that evening with him, Wayne, and some other dudes. According to Lamar's fairy tale, he had followed Wayne and me to North Hamilton Street, then watched from behind the ticket booth in the municipal parking lot across the street with his brother Stanley while Wayne and I supposedly broke in the front door. Lamar told investigators a car had pulled up, and an old lady got out and went inside, which could hardly be considered proof he was there, since it had been widely reported that Emma Crapser was murdered as she returned home from her bingo game that night. Lamar claimed he saw me and Wayne come running out the front door shortly after the old lady went inside. Wayne Moseley was also offered immunity and instant freedom in exchange for implicating me. He accepted the deal and immediately changed the story he originally gave to police back in 1977, about being home with his mother and knowing nothing about the murder (an account his mother had echoed under oath). Now Wayne was claiming I had kicked Ms. Crapser's legs out from under her and killed her when she walked in on the two of us while we were burglarizing her apartment. Wayne claimed he had run out the front door first and I had followed, then confronted Sweet Pea and yelled at him for screwing up as the lookout. All this commotion supposedly was going on right there in the street at eleven o'clock on a summer night, in view of the open bay of the ambulance service and across from a public parking lot. And the best witnesses the prosecution can produce are a couple of street thugs whose recollections change according to the size of the carrot dangling in front of them?

I was indicted for the murder. Elbert Pittman was indicted for burglary, but the statute of limitations had run out, and he wasn't charged. Wayne and Lamar would get their freedom once they testified in court against me.

What confounded me then and still does to this day is that I barely knew these guys—I'd only been in Poughkeepsie a few months back then in 1977, and they weren't my friends or, as far as I knew, my enemies. But they were happy as hell to railroad me and tell whatever lies investigators wanted to hear to shave a few years off their sentences. Didn't matter to them whether an innocent man died in prison or not.

Investigators had bagged three hundred to four hundred pieces of evidence from Ms. Crapser's apartment, plus some fingerprints and palm prints. The items they catalogued included a flashlight, a chisel, a pocketbook, a pair of women's shoes, a bankbook, white cord, a bottle, a tin can, a pair of cutting pliers, and a window frame with glass, taken from the bathroom. A thumbprint had been found on the inside of that window. The fingerprint evidence was among thirty-four items sent to the FBI; forensic analysts were asked to compare the prints to mine, Lamar Smith's, Wayne Moseley's, and Elbert Pittman's.

There were no matches.

The only thing tying me to the murder was the inconsistent testimony of Wayne Moseley, Lamar Smith, and Lamar's brother Stanley, who claimed that he and Lamar had seen me in Mansion Square Park and had followed me to North Hamilton, where they supposedly stood across the street and watched me messing with the door at number 15 just before eleven o'clock the night of Emma Crapser's murder. Stanley was crucial to the prosecution, my attorneys explained to me, because you need a second witness to back up any story provided by a criminal getting a deal in exchange for their testimony. Stanley's account made his brother's story admissible in court, and Lamar, of course, needed to testify to seal his deal with the prosecutor.

I had no alibi witnesses to offer the jury. My brother Tony had spent the night of June 14 at his girlfriend's, so he hadn't heard me come in. I didn't even know the name of the kid whose bike I rode home that night, and I never saw him again.

Nonetheless, Mickey and David felt certain that I would be acquitted: How could the jury *not* have reasonable doubt? No physical evidence, dubious eyewitnesses who had changed their stories to get favorable treatment from the prosecutor's office on separate convictions, and a motive that sounded lame from the get-go. I had been known to lift a stereo or two during my street days, and I can tell you right now that a ninety-two-year-old woman with a hear-

ing aid is not someone you think of targeting if you're l[
a boom box to fence.

What the jury didn't hear was that two young brothers with a history of violence had committed a similarly gruesome murder just months after the Crapser slaying, and only a few blocks away. Donald and Anthony Wise had confessed and were in prison when I was arrested and put on trial for a crime that matched their pattern to a T.

The Wises had been arrested in February 1978 for the murder of eighty-year-old Mary King during a burglary at the home she shared with her two sisters, who both survived the attack. Mrs. King was bound and gagged in similar grisly fashion as Emma Crapser had been eight months earlier, and their bodies were found in a similar position. The brothers were serving twenty-five years to life, each. Just before I went on trial—six years after Ms. Crapser was slain—the FBI finally compared the thumbprint on the inside of her bathroom window to the prints of convicted murderer Donald Wise.

They matched.

During my trial, Prosecutor William O'Neill argued that it proved nothing, that Wise could have been in Emma Crapser's apartment at any time, for any reason. He had a rap sheet for burglary. Besides, detectives had concluded the bathroom window was too small to be a likely point of entry or escape—a conclusion that overlooked how small Donald Wise was. O'Neill had also attacked the damning testimony by Madeline Dixon, Anthony Wise's girlfriend and the mother of his child. Madeline had told police that Anthony and Donald had walked her past the Crapser house a couple of weeks after the murder and told her that Donald had done a "movie" there—street slang for hurting someone—during a burglary. She recalled the Wise brothers also showed her a big brown leather purse filled with old coins and jewelry, which purportedly belonged to Emma Crapser. The jewelry and coins had later been sold or pawned, the girlfriend testified.

THREE WEEKS AFTER MY 1983 TRIAL BEGAN, the jury came back with its verdict on a Saturday afternoon. Some of the jurors were crying as they walked back into the courtroom, and none of them would look at me.

I was found guilty of murder in the second degree. The jurors were polled one by one to confirm that this was their verdict, and the reality hit me when I heard the twelfth yes.

"I didn't do no murder. I didn't commit no murder, man!" I shouted. "I tell you, I didn't commit no murder, man! What the fuck is going on? I didn't do no murder. Jesus Christ, Jesus Christ!"

The judge ordered the deputies standing by to remove me from the courtroom, but I kept hollering as they hustled me out.

"I didn't do no fucking murder. I didn't do no murder, man, I didn't kill no woman. God, I didn't commit no murder, didn't do it."

William O'Neill got into the elevator with me and the officers taking me away to jail. I looked at him with tears still streaming out of my eyes.

"You know I didn't do it," I said. "How can you live with yourself?"

The prosecutor bowed his head without saying a word. He couldn't look at me. The doors to the elevator opened, and I didn't see him again until my next trial.

TWO DAYS AFTER MY CONVICTION, a distraught Stanley Smith raced to the courthouse and recanted his testimony, not even asking for immunity for perjuring himself before the grand jury and on the witness stand during the trial. Stanley said he and Lamar had never seen me in the park that day, and they hadn't been on North Hamilton Street the night of the murder. They never witnessed me jiggling the lock on that front door or running out of the building afterward. He said his brother had pressured him to corroborate his story just so Lamar could get the promised deal and walk out of prison immediately, instead of serving out the three years left on his sentence. He would do anything for his brother, he apologized.

Stanley's admission came too late. The judge refused to overturn my conviction or order a new trial.

4

I REMEMBER ONE PERFECT DAY. It was the day I turned thirty-two. I already had spent eight birthdays behind bars, and though I didn't know it at the time, I would spend eighteen more. But the beauty of April 20, 1991, was forgetting that, all of that, for one single, blissful day.

Late April is when springtime peaks in the Hudson River Valley, like the high note in a favorite song. You get this soft patch of weather between the bone-cold winter and muggy hot summer, a perfect mix of breezy and warm, where you just want to turn your face to the sun and let your thoughts slip away like a kite cut free. I woke up feeling good, the kind of good that feels settled in for the day, so you know you'll be able to hold on to it for a while. After breakfast, I went out to the yard, headed for my usual workout. With boxing, you're always building on what you've got, pushing for better footwork, stronger hooks, more stamina. I was disciplined about my training, but on this particular day, I allowed myself the small luxury of getting distracted. On the way to the weights, something out of the ordinary caught my eye on the ground ahead. From a distance, I could tell that it was yellow, but what it was, I couldn't make out. I decided to investigate. When I was a few steps away, I laughed when I recognized the unfamiliar sight.

It was a flower.

I stooped down and plucked it, decided it was mine, a little birthday present blossoming in the hard dirt of a prison yard. I wandered over to the handball court and lay down on the warm concrete, using my workout clothes for a pillow. I put the yellow flower in my lap and closed my eyes, enjoying the sunshine. I heard footsteps and heard a familiar voice, my man Cisco.

"Yo, man, happy birthday," he greeted me. I'd forgotten mentioning it to him and felt gratified that he had remembered.

Pretty soon, the other guys I usually worked out with came looking for me.

Yo, man, what you doing? Why aren't you working out?

"It's my birthday," I announced, again and again.

Happy birthday. Happy birthday, man. Yo, happy birthday.

One of the Carribean dudes who ran a little carryout restaurant from his cell told me to drop by later for a meal.

Back on the gallery, my run of good luck continued when I saw that the CO on duty was one of the friendlier, more laid-back officers who knew I wasn't a troublemaker and sometimes cut me some slack. It was the other cellblock's day for the movies, not mine, but I asked if I could go, anyway, and he gave me the nod. I grabbed a shower and put on my dress shirt and best pair of state-issued green pants before heading to the chapel, which doubled as the Sing Sing Cineplex. It was always funny, in a twisted-up kind of way, to sit there watching some movie knowing that whatever bad thing happened on-screen—bank heist, shooting, a car chase—a fair number of the guys sitting with you in the audience had probably done worse. People always had opinions afterward about how something really would have gone down, or what a bad guy should've done to avoid getting caught. As if they were experts on that subject.

During rec, a group of Muslims I knew beckoned me over, and their leader surprised me with a yellow cake he had baked for me in the mess hall. They all sang "Happy Birthday," and we spent the rest of our time outside eating and talking and laughing as if we were picnicking in a park instead of a prison yard. Back inside, I went to claim my free birthday dinner from the friend who'd offered to cook for me. He greeted me with a big helping of canned jack mackerel with rice and yams. I took it back to my cell and sat listening to music on my little portable stereo while I ate my fill. Everybody had made my day good. I had celebrated, and I felt proud of myself for making the best of the worst. The prison sounds of night faded in the background, becoming a white-noise lullaby of keys jangling, cell doors shutting, men's voices rising and falling.

On my thirty-second birthday, I went to sleep happy.

5

THE BOXING RING WAS IN THE ABANDONED DEATH HOUSE, right over where the electric chair used to be. You could still see the hole in the ground where they had taken it out, but it didn't bother me one bit. We had staked our claim, and we were going to turn this notorious room into our refuge, a sweat-equity workshop for rebuilding ruined lives.

The man behind this vision was Sergeant Bob Jackson—a ruddy-faced CO who trained boxing champs on the outside first at the old Gramercy Gym and then at the famed Gleason's in Brooklyn. In 1985, word started making its way around the cellblocks that Jackson had permission from the superintendent to form a prison boxing team. At first, the other COs balked, protesting that it would just make aggressive men even more dangerous and give them lessons, no less, in how to better overpower prison staff. But Jackson was adamant and used the respect he'd built over his twenty-year career in the prison system to persuade the naysayers, arguing that the focus and self-discipline the sport demanded would make his boxers the best-behaved inmates in Sing Sing. I was one of the first ones in line to sign up. I went down to the first floor of the prison hospital, where Jackson was interviewing candidates, and tried to make my case. I told him about my brief time with Floyd Patterson, and how I'd stuck to my workout routine since getting locked up.

"How much time you got?" he wanted to know.

"I got twenty years to life."

Jackson was shrewd enough to know what kind of crime likely went with that kind of sentence. I could feel his pale blue eyes sizing me up. I could feel my heart racing. I wanted this. I needed this.

"Why should I put you on?" he asked.

"Listen, you put me on this boxing team, you don't have to worry about me," I pleaded. "Just give me a chance."

"If you're on the team, you gotta stay out of trouble," he warned me.

I nodded. I was in.

A dozen of us on the team were tasked with turning the old Death House into a gym. There was no roof on the old building, and it was now a crumbling ruin with deadwood, twisted metal, and other debris from its last incarnation as a vocational shop. The last of the 614 inmates executed at Sing Sing—more than at any other prison in the country—had been electrocuted on August 15, 1963. Sing Sing had housed some of the most notorious criminals in the world, people like Julius and Ethel Rosenberg, Willie Sutton, Lucky Luciano, and members of Murder Inc., a Brooklyn gang responsible for at least twenty homicides. Some of us on the boxing team likely would have met the same gruesome fate if New York hadn't abolished the death penalty.

We'd gather in the yard to work out in the morning, then we were allowed to go through the gates to the adjoining field to continue our workout with Bob Jackson. Only afterward, in the afternoon, would we do our boxing—hitting the bags, jumping rope, sparring. Spider, Sun God, Whisper, Omar, Big Red and Big Black, Macho, and Salladin, the six-foot-five welterweight, and I spent a whole year just training.

Boxing became my peace, my salvation, my pain reliever, and my strength. I used it to get rid of my anger, to purge all the hurt and pain and frustration boiling up inside me. Everybody who had been in my life before—my family, my lovers, my friends—was gone, either taken away or pushed away or run away or drifted away. I was by myself. I put on a good show of seeming tough, too cool to give a damn, but I felt lonely on the inside.

Training was all about conditioning myself. I would run three or four miles every day. When I ran or hit the bag or did my jumping jacks, my five hundred sit-ups, or my military push-ups, I had to concentrate, focusing my mind on what I wanted my body to do. I had to command myself to do better, work harder, get stronger. I had to learn how to breathe right. *You don't prepare yourself for the punch,* Jackson taught us, *you prepare yourself for the fight.*

Sparring with my teammates, I ended up with a few black eyes and got dazed, but I never got knocked out. I've never been laid out on the floor.

The first time I sparred with Spider, we were going at it real good when Spider got me with a hook that hit my nose and knocked it back into place. It'd been crooked since it was busted in street fights when I was a kid. "Thank you, man!" I said as I hopped out of the ring. It took two weeks for it to heal, but Spider did as fine a nose job as any plastic surgeon could've.

When we weren't conditioning our bodies, we were priming our minds. Bob Jackson would show us films of all the greats— Sugar Ray Robinson, Larry Holmes, Jack Dempsey. I tried to steal moves like the mean jab that made Héctor Comacho famous, or the fast dancing of lightweight Pernell Whitaker, who was so slippery his opponents could hardly land a blow. I even had ideas about creating my own signature moves.

I pushed myself even harder on my calisthenics, the soreness in my muscles giving way to strength as I got bigger and bigger. I denied myself the junk food I usually snacked on—cheddar chips, cupcakes, candy bars, honeybuns. Jackson got us little extras, like orange juice and V8s. Sometimes I'd fast to help me tone up. I felt myself getting healthier. My eyes were sharper. My mind was clear and calm. My rope work and footwork improved until finally I felt ready to make my debut.

"Okay, everybody gets to see what I been working on," I announced one day. Spider stepped into the ring with me and right away threw his killer jab. I stepped over and hit him with a body shot and cracked his ribs with the first punch.

"Next," I said.

Every man on the team had his particular strength. Whisper, a middleweight, was known for his speed. Big Red was tough as nails, a heavyweight. There was Muhammad Aziz, a light-heavyweight pro with an 18-0 record, a stick-and-move fighter who used to spar with me. One of my trainers was Carlos, an inmate who had once been on the Cuban boxing team. In six months, he had me doing ten-punch combinations. My signature punch was from the southpaw stance, right hand to the left side of the body. I knew I did it right if I made a guy twitch or crumble to the floor or something ended up broken. That's why I loved that punch. If you can't take my right hand, that ain't my fault, that's your fault.

In the ring, you have to hide pain. You learn how to conceal your hurt.

Sparring was tough. That kid who could never stand to lose a basketball or baseball game burst out from inside me, and I quickly got a reputation for being fiercely competitive. I made some enemies, but I could tell Bob Jackson was impressed. That mattered more.

One guy wanted to fight me because I stung him in a sparring session, and I could tell he wanted to turn it into a war.

"Hey, man, you wanna go there, I'll go there," I told him. I wasn't one to start anything, but I wasn't about to back down, either. We went at it. He let one go on me, I let one go on him. We went four and a half rounds before Bob Jackson stopped us in the middle of it. He could see we were starting to get real serious.

"Keep whatever you do in the ring," he admonished us as we glared at each other angrily. "Don't take it outta the ring."

We took his warning seriously; none of us ever fought outside the ring, because we knew Bob Jackson would throw us off the team, and if that happened, we'd most likely get transferred out of Sing Sing.

MY LIFE IN THE POPULATION WAS CHANGING around the same time I joined the boxing team. I'd taken my GED test just to have something to do right after I'd started my bid, and I'd passed it straightaway. But there were no social workers or counselors to talk to you about continuing your education, so for my first two years in Sing Sing, I did nothing with my life except hang out with Jose and get high.

Maybe it was the reefer or just the loneliness, but I stupidly ended up telling Jose my story, breaking the most basic prison survival rule. There's always somebody looking to make use of your misery. You gotta be real cool with a guy to talk about your crime. You never know who's going to try to get out of jail by twisting your story to their advantage. I knew that better than anyone; I was there in the first place because some punk-ass teenager bought his freedom by telling a fat lie about me. Anyway, I was ashamed to be in prison on a murder charge. But I shared my story, and before I knew it, some dude came back and let on that some rapist was busy running his mouth about how I had murdered a ninety-two-year-old woman, trying to justify his crime by saying I'd done way worse. I angrily confronted Jose.

"Yo, from now on, this friendship is done. If my name comes out of your mouth again, I'll whip your ass."

I eventually forgave him, but it was years before I trusted anyone again.

There was one group at Sing Sing whose crimes we knew because of the sentences they served: the lifers. I had noticed a tight clique of them out in the yard. They were Muslims who kept to themselves, holding themselves somehow apart and above the day-to-day drama and nonsense that swirled around in the prison's general population. One day, when we were coming back in from the yard, a lifer named Shariff stopped me.

"Can I talk to you?" he asked politely.

"Sure," I said. Shariff was an older guy, quiet and contemplative. He seemed to be an anchor among the devout Muslims from what I could tell—the type of convict who earned his respect through wisdom instead of intimidation.

"You're fronting," he told me simply.

"What you mean, man?" I demanded.

"It's a façade you're putting out there," Shariff went on. "It's not you."

I shook my head. "Man, I ain't trying to hear that," I scoffed. Shariff pressed ahead.

"Listen, man, I'm seeing a different man than the one you're showing," he insisted. "What're you going to do with your time? What're you going to do with your life? Are you going to spend it just playing basketball with nothing to show in the end? You know what you're around here? You're around doctors, lawyers, businessmen, people who were involved in real estate. You can make this place a university of learning!"

Shariff was sensing in me a hunger whose pangs I was barely beginning to feel. I had tuned out so completely that things I used to be passionate about didn't even register anymore. I didn't even notice when the World Series was on TV in the rec area. Shariff caught me at the right time; he could tell I had flattened out. I had reached a turning point, without realizing at the time that the changes I was ready to make weren't just incremental, but monumental. If I had been a religious man then, I suppose I would have recognized that God put Shariff in my path that day for a reason.

It took a stint in keep-lock to seal the deal. Keep-lock is just what it sounds like: you're kept locked in your cell twenty-three hours a day as punishment for breaking a rule. I had disobeyed a direct order from a CO who had ordered me to return to my cell when I was busy socializing with my buddies out on the gallery.

Other folks may talk about having a big epiphany when an angel appears before them or they have some terrifying brush with death, but mine? My big transformation came because of a freakin' cigarette. It's never, ever, *ever* the big thing that makes you explode in the joint.

A guy who was supposed to be cool with me was walking past my cell while I was in keep-lock, and I called out to him to ask for a cigarette. In keep-lock, I couldn't get to the commissary, or do any of my usual bartering out on the galleries.

"I ain't got any," said this guy who was supposed to have my back.

"What you mean?" I couldn't believe he was denying me this small favor that I would've done for him straightaway, no questions asked. A pack of cigarettes was worth all of a dollar.

"Yo, you got a pack right there in your pocket, man. I can see it! You know when I get out, I'll get mine and pay you back."

He shook his head. Maybe he'd got an attitude because it was a new pack and man, you hafta make it last, and no one ever gives him shit so why should he give me a cigarette? I wouldn't let it go, though.

"That's how you going to do me? It's right there in your damn pocket! C'mon, bro!"

Dude shot me shade like I was some beggar on the street, that pathetic, and grudgingly reached for his pack, shaking out a smoke. "Man," he muttered in a way that cut me down even lower.

The way he handed over that single cigarette made me feel ashamed. Right then and there I had my epiphany. Silently, I cursed myself.

Man, you got prune wine underneath your bed, reefer on top of your cabinet, you're acting like you're on the streets, like you don't even care. What's wrong with you? You've become an animal. Nothing more than an animal. Who's the master? You or the damn cigarette? Cigarettes don't control me; I control the cigarettes. Enough is enough, man.

All these negative thoughts started crashing down on me then, all the hurt there'd been in my life—my father and mother, my brothers and sisters, my ex-girlfriend Stephanie. I let it all soak in, and I realized with some surprise that I'd had my fill of feeling sorry for myself.

Right then and there, I took that cigarette and crushed it and threw it in the toilet bowl.

"That's it," I said aloud. "I'm done."

And the funny thing is, from that day on, I was. I stopped drinking, stopped smoking, stopped getting high, and stopped hanging out with Jose, who got so mad that he wanted to fight me over abandoning him. "You full of baloney, man, just like the rest of them," he told me. "You'll be back. You'll come back."

But I didn't.

I started spending time with Shariff and his crew, and they introduced me to the world of academic and self-improvement programs that religious groups, nonprofits, and the state offered to inmates. The chapel, it turned out, was a schoolhouse when services weren't being held. For the first time in my life, I started feeding my mind instead of numbing it. I studied economics, business, theater, speech, theology, peer counseling, food services. When a new opportunity came up, I signed up. I began devouring any motivational and self-help books I could lay my hands on. I copied page after page, longhand, into composition books so I would have the words of wisdom to keep in case the book itself ever got confiscated or lost or loaned to someone who got transferred out of Sing Sing before he could return it. Flip through my stacks of notebooks, and you would have found investment advice from Donald Trump crammed up against the writings of Malcolm X. I knew in my heart that I would be exonerated someday, that I had to be, but I no longer wanted freedom alone. I wanted a future. I knew that education was the key, and that Shariff was right: Sing Sing could open my mind.

It was the boxing, I know, that gave me the ability to concentrate with an intensity I had never known before. Prison wasn't going to confine me; it was going to be my liberation.

One of the first courses I enrolled in was the year-long program to become certified as a paralegal. Mickey Steiman had been so worried by my breakdown in court when I heard the guilty verdict that he had gotten the jail doc to prescribe me Thorazine and put me on suicide watch. My despair had gradually hardened into determination, and even though I trusted Mickey to keep working on my case, I was keen to learn as much about the law as I could on my own, too. I began spending time in the prison's small law library, studying the different grounds for appeal and poring over case histories. The library was a small room with a few tables and old manual typewriters. It was run by a lawyer named Steve who was doing time for embezzling more than a million dollars. Steve was nothing but patient and kind to the barely literate criminals who struggled to decipher Ivy League textbooks with their dense citations, opinions, and case studies. It was never simple or straightforward. You would have to wade across the sucking mudhole of fifty pages or more to get the answer to what you thought was a quick question. All that legal jargon could deflate even an avid reader like me, but over time, it became my second language. Steve showed me how to file a motion, and I filed them all the way up to the U.S. Supreme Court. Every single one was denied. Each time, I would hit the law library again. Books commanded my attention now, and I gorged like the starving man I was. I set my sights on earning a college degree. I had always been street-smart, but my intellect had been left unfed. Discovering a capacity to learn, when you're already a grown man, is a gift straight from God: you spend a lifetime shuffling around and then find out you can run like Jesse Owens.

WITH NO FAMILY OR FRIENDS ON THE OUTSIDE with the means or the inclination to send me packages or put money in my canteen account, I got myself on the inmate payroll. My preferred job was being a porter, even though the five or six dollars I earned a week was chump change compared to something like working the mess hall, where you started at fourteen dollars and could go up to twenty-five a week. If you completed training and got certified, you could make as much as thirty-five, forty dollars a week as an assistant cook. As a porter, I just had to clean the gallery floor. The COs got to know me better, and once they saw I wasn't a troublemaker, they'd cut me a little slack now and then, like giving me permission to take a shower when my cellblock was out in the yard or when I came back from boxing. Some of the officers would let me hang out on the gallery when we were supposed to be in our cells, as long as I locked back in if the lookouts on the next gallery sent word that a supervisor was on his way. There was an unspoken code of honor not just among inmates, but between inmates and COs, as well: you protected your officer out of respect; you had his back like he had yours. Both sides looked the other way when it was mutually beneficial—if you were violating a stack of rules by running a carryout chicken joint from your cell, for example, you would be well advised to regularly feed the COs assigned to your gallery for free. The hard-core drug dealers still orchestrating their businesses on the outside knew which officers to pay off on the inside; a few COs, including a lieutenant, ended up getting busted for trafficking. It played the other way, too: if a CO showed a cruel streak, or went out of his or her way to jam up somebody, payback was going to happen sooner or later. The lucky ones just got a bucket of warm piss sloshed at them when they walked past a certain cell; the seriously unlucky ones ended up on disability. All it took was a smashed lightbulb in a dark corridor and a few guys waiting with a blanket to throw over your head so you couldn't testify later about who had jumped you and stomped on your rib cage till it snapped like balsa wood.

My prison hustle was fairly common, and harmless enough

that COs were willing to let it ride as long as I was cool about it. I expanded my little store to include chicken and hamburgers. You could buy the raw protein from a middleman with mess hall connections. I could even get frozen french fries and cooking oil. It wasn't that hard then to rig a little hot plate by dismembering and crossing some wires on one of those cheap plastic electric kettles that were supposed to boil water for coffee or tea but barely made it past lukewarm. After all those years of being denied food by my foster parents, I took comfort in knowing that I had more than enough to eat in prison, that I wouldn't have to feel hunger pangs ever again. I kept my sodas cold in a cooler I made out of an old box, some styrofoam, and plastic bags. I would pay a guy who worked in the mess hall two or three packs of cigarettes a week to deliver stolen ice. Just pop it in my cooler, slide it under my bed, and it'd last for a few days. As luck would have it, my cell was in what you could call a prime retail location—right around the corner from the block where most of the reefer was sold. I did a lot of business with stoners who had the munchies.

Every so often, the COs would yell "Lock down!" for a surprise inspection of cells. There was always the risk that I would lose my shop and have to start from scratch again.

"Bozella, you know you're not supposed to have this shit," the CO would say.

"Man, I got a store, man, what'm I gonna do? Here, take a candy bar. I'll get you a meal later."

Some officers were easy and would leave you be. Someone like me was hardly worth the trouble of writing up. What I had in my cell was nothing compared to the stockpiles of illegal or dangerous or just plain crazy shit other inmates hustled. One guy even had a working police scanner under his bunk.

The only way Sing Sing's underground microeconomy could thrive the way it did back then was through a gentlemen's agreement among more than a thousand convicted felons: be respectful. Like I've said before, respect is everything in prison, and it is constantly being scrutinized, quantified, and, above all, enforced.

Disrespecting a CO might rate a Tier One, or low-level, infraction according to Sing Sing's official disciplinary guidelines, but dissing a fellow inmate could get you the death penalty according to the unofficial code of conduct among the prisoners. The bottom line is this: one guy can fuck it up for everyone. Say the CO in charge hears that his lieutenant is on his way to the gallery, which is supposed to be clear, but everybody's been behaving today so the CO hasn't hassled us to stay in our cells. But now his ass is on the line, so he calls out for everyone to lock in, but you ignore his order. When he sees you disrespecting him that way, he gets fired up and charges through the gallery slamming all the cell doors shut. And maybe six guys who were getting high in a cell at the opposite end of the block didn't hear all this commotion, and now they get caught by surprise when the CO appears. Now the CO is so pissed, he calls for backup and tosses every single cell. All kinds of contraband ends up getting seized. At the end of the day, the homies are pissed because six of their guys are locked in the box in the Special Housing Unit, known as SHU, on solitary and facing new charges, and everyone else is pissed because they don't have their drugs or knives anymore. And all this happened because you wouldn't lock in, because you had to grandstand. So the word from the box is "get him." What do you think is going to happen to you when you go out to the yard? You think anyone is going to back you up now? Look what your stupid mistake cost you and everybody else. All you had to do was step inside your cell and mind your own damn business for five minutes. You made the worst mistake you can make in here. You forgot where you are. What you do has consequences for everyone. You're just one stupid fuck of a domino.

I ADJUSTED TO PRISON LIFE and the deadly society I found myself in, but I never accepted it. Boxing gave me something to dedicate myself to, and the better I got, the more I allowed myself to dream about winning the ultimate fight, for my freedom. When Bob Jackson brought Golden Gloves light heavyweight champ Lou "Honey Boy" Del Valle in for a fight against me, the feral energy usually crackling through the prison turned almost buoyant. I was just one of twelve inmates scheduled to fight that afternoon at the prison gym, but I had the most at stake. If I won this bout, Sing Sing would have its own Golden Gloves champion. Goodwill greeted me wherever I turned from the minute I sat down for my light fight-day breakfast of cereal and eggs. *Good luck, yo, man, good luck, good luck! Go whup his ass, man!* Inmates and COs alike were excited about the fights, and I was one of the main-event guys. I spent the hours I had to kill until the match reading a book on boxing and looking at the ring, envisioning how I would fight, what I would do. Honey Boy, I knew, was a southpaw, and that was going to affect my usual strategy. Finally, it was time, and as I stood next to my opponent, waiting to be announced, I quickly sized him up. He was a little shorter than me. *I'm going to knock this dude out,* I mentally assured myself. I'd played it all nonchalant when Bob Jackson had first told me I was going up against a Golden Glove ("Hey, I don't care"), but the truth was I was anxious to prove how good I was. When the bell rang, we both fought very hard, and I was able to get him with a couple of good jabs. It felt like we were on equal ground. But then the first round tipped in my favor and I went into the second round overconfident. I knew I was tough and could take a punch, but he hadn't gotten me yet. He came at me, but I hit him with a body shot and knew I hurt him when I heard him let out a surprised "oooh." *I got him, I got him now,* I silently crowed. I was coming off a jab near the end of the second round when he came at me with his head instead of his hand, catching me off guard enough to connect with a three-punch combo that turned my head gear. I could feel it scrape the right side of my skull, but I felt fine. It wasn't until the third round that the blood suddenly came pouring down my face. The ref blew the whistle and stopped the fight.

"Yo, man, please just give me thirty more seconds," I begged. "Let me go out there for thirty more seconds." I was sure I could triumph if I just had half a minute more.

"Sorry, ABA rules," the ref said. He stopped the fight, and that's how Del Valle won. We shook hands and agreed it was a good fight. I was still determined to get in a final jab, though.

"Yo, man, you got away with that one," I told him. Del Valle let me have that and gave me his phone number, inviting me to call him from the inside if I wanted to talk sometime. I kept in sporadic touch for a year or so, calling him collect at his grandma's house. I eventually stopped calling, though; I didn't want his reputation to get tarnished in any way by befriending a convict, for one thing. But it also hurt like hell to press up against that window of what my life could have been. Both Bob Jackson and I realized after that bout that I had the genuine potential to go pro if I ever got the chance. It seemed unlikely I ever would.

The Sing Sing team would fight amateur clubs and other prisons, and I became famous as the guy no one could knock out. It earned me a new kind of respect, one that came out of being admired instead of just feared. I became the light-heavyweight champion of Sing Sing and was awarded a championship belt crafted by a fellow inmate. The sense of pride that came from achieving something and having that achievement acknowledged was new to me. I thought about all the opportunities I had squandered when I was younger—all the different programs and education available to me when I was in the foster-care system—and I knew that even though I was innocent, I was still partly responsible for my circumstances. I was the one who chose the street over the classroom, who surrounded myself with sketchy criminals instead of righteous men. Self-pity wasn't my tune, but I did feel sorry as hell for the boy I had been, for that unwanted kid who had taken a foolish turn down the wrong path.

NOT LONG AFTER MY FIGHT WITH LOU DEL VALLE, a CO came to tell me I had a phone call. Mickey and David were on the line with news so good I thought they were bullshitting me: one of their numerous legal maneuvers to try to get my guilty verdict thrown out had finally worked. They had gotten hold of notes my prosecutors had made during jury selection. Out of a pool of 275 potential jurors, there had been only six black people. One had been excused, and the prosecution systematically dismissed the other five. A judge agreed that I had been denied my constitutional right to a jury of my peers, and seven years into my sentence, a new trial was ordered in November 1990.

Before we went to court, though, I had some unresolved business to tend to in the cellblocks. Donald and Anthony Wise had been transferred to Sing Sing to serve their time for the slaying of Mary King, the eighty-year-old woman who had been beaten and suffocated with cloth stuffed down her throat just like Emma Crapser. My defense team planned to bring up the striking similarities between the King attacks and the one on Ms. Crapser, and to point out again that the FBI had concluded that the fingerprint found on the inside of Ms. Crapser's broken bathroom window belonged to Donald Wise. Likewise, the description of the bogus plumber who had been inside Ms. Crapser's apartment earlier that afternoon matched Donald Wise. There was not one shred of evidence placing me in that apartment or linking me to the murder.

Even though I was doing time for a murder that evidence strongly suggested Donald Wise had committed, I bore no particular grudge against him. Don't get me wrong: he was one foul cat. But he wasn't the one who had concocted the big lie and then borne false witness against me in court. I held Wayne Moseley and Lamar and Stanley Smith accountable for that. And more than anyone, I blamed the Poughkeepsie police and the Dutchess County prosecutors for the injustice done to me. That said, if I didn't handle this delicate situation with Wise just right, I could end up with a prison label far worse than murderer: snitch. I had to let Wise know what was going down.

One day out in the yard, I had a brother watch my back while I approached the Wises. They were, as usual, together. I'd heard that Donald had become Buddhist, while Anthony was Muslim. We saw each other every day but had never spoken.

"Yo, man, you know who I am?" I asked now.

Donald nodded once. I could sense him tighten just slightly, getting on point for whatever came next. I would have done the same.

"I just want you to know, my case been overturned."

Both of them looked at me, waiting. I held their stare and kept talking. I knew it was critical that I come across as neutral but direct. They didn't bother asking what you would think an innocent man would—why my business had anything to do with them—because we all knew why.

"I just want you to know, I got a new trial and your name is likely to come up," I went on. "Nobody's looking to jam you up here, but I gotta do what I gotta do. I'm not gonna sit up there and point a finger, so don't go around talking about me like a dog, like I did something to you, like a snitch. I don't want any problems."

They considered this for a moment, then Donald spoke up.

"Naw, ain't no problems," he said.

I tried not to get my hopes up too much about the second trial. One jury already had convicted me on the word of a couple of juvenile delinquents who were persuaded to testify in exchange for their own freedom. Would a second jury see through the bald-faced lies? Mickey and David felt confident that an acquittal was within grasp. Besides the similar attacks on three elderly white sisters within a few months and less than a mile from the Crapser murder—and the trail of evidence and witnesses that led straight to Donald Wise—my lawyers were also itching to kick giant holes in the credibility of prosecutor William O'Neill's star witnesses. None of them had so much as mentioned me when they were questioned as possible suspects right after the murder, but once O'Neill's team pointed the finger at me and then offered them sweetheart deals on jail terms they were already serving, it was game on, and the lies got so tangled up even the liars couldn't keep them straight. Lamar Smith's own brother, Stanley, was the only one to feel even a tinge of remorse about what he had done to me, but his perjury confession two days after my conviction didn't undo the damage.

Now Stanley was willing to admit in open court that he had lied on the stand during my first trial when he claimed to have been watching from across the street with Lamar while Wayne Moseley and I supposedly broke into the Crapser house on North Hamilton. No one was offering Stanley immunity for betraying his brother; he was running the very real risk of being charged with perjury or obstruction of justice.

To say the police investigation into Emma Crapser's murder was shoddy would be generous. It was a cartoon. All they did was lazily round up "the usual suspects" from the street—Lamar Smith being one of the first—and then fixate on their scapegoat—me— without any regard for evidence, procedure, or simple logic. They indicted me before they bothered to run the fingerprint evidence on the inside of the victim's bathroom window. And they conveniently destroyed or lost taped interviews we could have used in my defense, like those with Lamar Smith originally denying any knowledge of the crime and providing a verified alibi that he was at McDonald's when it happened. Wayne Moseley and Lamar Smith testified at this second trial, their convoluted lies losing and adding various embellishments from the first time they had spun their tale. At one point during a recess, I was left in the courtroom with Wayne Moseley. I stood up and glared at him. He refused to look at me.

Donald and Anthony Wise were both subpoenaed for the 1990 trial and both took the Fifth Amendment against self-incrimination. It had been thirteen years since the murder itself, and many of the people who originally gave statements to police—neighbors, street people—had either moved away or passed away. Anthony's girlfriend at the time, Madeline Dixon (later Madeline South), had died. Despite all the obstacles and frustrations, though, the second trial went so well that we were in an upbeat mood once the jury went to deliberate. Even the judge seemed to think it was a slam dunk in my favor, remarking out loud that the jurors would probably return with a not-guilty verdict within an hour. She questioned why prosecutors had even bothered to bring the case to trial.

Hearing that, O'Neill quickly left the room, then shortly after that summoned Mickey Steiman. District Attorney William Grady was ready to play let's make a deal. An acquittal would be a huge black eye for the D.A. in such a sensational case and would also move one more murder into the "unsolved" column during his term in office. Reopening and reinvestigating a case thirteen years after the crime occurred would no doubt cost the county a good chunk of money and manpower. It looked to us like Grady wanted to save face and avoid the headache of trying to solve a cold case.

"Plead guilty to manslaughter in exchange for a sentence that would make you immediately eligible for parole," Mickey came back and relayed to me.

I shot it down as soon as I heard the word *guilty*.

"I didn't kill anyone, and I'm not going to say I did," I said.

Mickey carried the news back to the prosecutors, who instantly upped the ante. Mickey approached me again with the newest offer.

"Guilty to manslaughter and immediate freedom."

Same answer, I told him. It wasn't even tempting to me. I'd been in prison for nearly seven years already and dreamed every single damn day of getting out and becoming a pro boxer, of pursuing my education, of getting married, of raising a family of my own, of having a real life. I would have given just about anything for all that.

Except my name.

I didn't care if it took twenty minutes or twenty years or my lifetime: my name had to be cleared.

This go-around, Grady indicated he would consider something called an Alford-Serrano plea. An Alford plea is one where you don't admit doing the crime, but you agree that the prosecution has enough evidence to establish guilt. Before I could wrap my head around the Alford option, though, the bailiff interrupted us.

The verdict was in.

Once again, I watched a jury file back into the courtroom without meeting my eyes. I knew what that meant.

"In the matter of the People of the State of New York against Dewey R. Bozella, we find the defendant guilty . . ."

This time, my legs stayed strong, not buckling beneath me, and I held back the bitter tears.

"Are you serious?" I asked. "You can't be serious!"

When I stood later before the judge, waiting to be sentenced, I asked to read a four-page statement I had written out by hand in my prison cell.

"I stand here strong with the faith of God that one day I will be free," I read. "I recognize that you may have my physical body, but you don't have my mind and spirit."

I thanked Mickey and David for fighting for me and begged them not to feel bad about losing in court, because "people in our day and time are deaf and don't want to listen to the truth, and dumb to their own blindness, and don't know what is going on, or [sic] too damn scared to stand up for what's right."

I went on for some time about the history of racism in America, and how it demanded now that a black man be punished for a white woman's murder regardless of the facts. I offered sarcastic regards to William O'Neill, "for he has to be a hell of a man to go to sleep with a smile on his face and then wake up in the morning and say, 'Job well done,' on taking away my life twice.

"If there was ever a case in the County of Dutchess that showed inconsistency, lies, and reasonable doubt, this is it. So, if you wonder how I feel? I feel let down and destroyed by my own human race."

I recounted how I had used my time in prison to box, participate in various workshops, earn my paralegal certificate, and pursue a college degree. I was even learning how to speak Japanese and read Arabic.

"The hurt and letdowns of life have just made me stronger," I told the court.

"I know there is no justice when I have to pay the price for someone else's crime," I concluded. "As a man, I'll make the best of the worst because I refuse to be weak and wicked and become a coward to that which I know is right."

The judge sentenced me, once again, to twenty years to life.

"I didn't do Miss Crapser's murder, and you know I didn't do Miss Crapser's murder," I protested. I knew my words didn't matter, but it felt important to say them, to keep saying them, until my truth was acknowledged.

"I wasn't there, sir," the judge responded as the deputies escorted me from the courtroom. "That's all. Thank you."

But it wasn't all. It couldn't be.

6

WHO DOESN'T DREAM OF ESCAPE? When your mind is the only part of you still free, it tugs at you now and then, urging you to find a way to follow it out of this place, out of your imprisonment. I heard of a couple guys who tried to break out of Sing Sing while I was there, but the details were always hazy on the cellblock grapevine, and the bottom line is that no one succeeded. They don't call it maximum security for a joke. I remember one dude supposedly slipped out through a window down at the school building and made it all the way past the fences, using coats or a blanket to cover the barbed wire. He got caught at the old railroad tracks that cut through the far edge of the prison grounds. On the rare occasion when I would let my daydreams drift to escape, the practical side of my nature would jump right in and push back hard, the voice of reason haranguing me back to cruel reality: *Where you going to go if you make it past the razor wire and the dogs and guards?* the voice demanded. *How you going to find money, food, a roof over your head? You got nobody.*

My loneliness was a chronic ache, a muffled drumbeat in the

background of my life. It wasn't that I didn't feel the pain; I was just used to it. If you wanted to knock me down with an emotional blow, it took a sucker punch to get the job done. The first one came back when I'd been locked up for a year. A CO had come to my cell one day just before lunch, after I'd finished working out.

"They want you down at the chapel," he said.

"Why?" I wondered.

"The reverend would like to see you."

"The reverend wants to see me? What for?" I was starting to feel the dread build inside me. I wasn't involved in any kind of religious activity then, and I didn't even know the chaplain. A summons like this could not mean anything good. It was a long walk to the chapel, down the A block and across two football fields. I tried to hope it wasn't news of a death awaiting me when I arrived at the reverend's office. He greeted me kindly.

"How you doing?"

"Okay," I answered tentatively. I tried to brace myself for whatever was coming. He told me to sit down, then got straight to the point.

"Your brother Tony, he passed away. Would you like to make a phone call?"

I called Allen Thomas, and Leon answered.

"Tony was shot in the head," Leon told me. Tony had been in his car. Police were saying it was a drug deal gone bad, but I knew instantly that Tony was collateral damage. He was nowhere near like me. Tony was a Good Samaritan, not a street thug. He worked with street kids, and more than likely had been trying to save some lost soul when he stuck his nose in the wrong business. Leon said the cops had arrested the guys who did it.

"Don't tell me any names," I warned Leon. I had already let

Stanley Jackson slide for killing our brother Ernie, and I knew I couldn't do it twice. If Tony's killers got convicted and ended up at Sing Sing, as they easily could have, I couldn't afford to know.

After we hung up, the chaplain asked if I wanted to attend Tony's funeral, and he promised to make arrangements for me to go. I took the long walk back to my cell. I remember sitting down on my bed and being very calm—before I went berserk. Two brothers murdered. I tore my fucking cell up. I threw the locker across the room, turned the bed upside down. I let all the rage inside me out. A couple of COs came around. "You all right?" one asked. "You all right?"

"I'm going to be all right, man, just leave me the fuck alone."

They left without ordering me to clean up my cell or writing me up for the outburst. Inmates started coming back from lunch and paused when they passed my trashed cell. "You all right?" people kept asking.

"Yeah, just need some time alone."

I spent from noon until late that night just sitting there, staring at the floor. Finally I asked for a mop and broom to clean out my cell before going to bed. If I dreamed, my dreams all escaped before dawn.

When the day of Tony's funeral arrived, two officers came to escort me to the service in Poughkeepsie. "Listen, man, when we get to the funeral, promise not to try to escape," they said.

"Yeah, I promise."

I was allowed to say good-bye to my brother unshackled. The room was packed, and my eyes scanned the crowd, not finding the faces I sought. Where were my brothers Michael and Albert? And Leon? The only sibling I spotted was my sister Lisa, whom I barely knew. When the service ended, the officers told me I could have a few minutes with my family. Lisa and I hugged. Then it was time to go back to Sing Sing. Prisoners weren't allowed to attend burials—being out in the wide open like that was considered too great an escape risk.

SOME TIME AFTER MY SECOND TRIAL, Leon came up from the city to see me and I hardly recognized the strapping man in front of me.

"Yo, man, I'm boxing now," Leon had boasted. "I went to the Golden Gloves. I lost but I had my first fight, and I'm feeling good." I thought the pride swelling my heart would bust my chest wide open. Leon had turned out okay, thanks to his surrogate father, Allen Thomas. He looked good and was making something of his life.

My own boxing days had come to a frustrating end after my recent trial, which had kept me locked up in Poughkeepsie and away from Sing Sing for about year. When I got processed back to Sing Sing, I discovered that budget cuts and the imminent retirement of Bob Jackson had caused the boxing program to wither away. A few of us from the old team tried to get it going again with another sergeant and a promise of help from world welterweight champ Buddy McGirt, but it just didn't come through.

Leon and Allen Thomas came to visit again in 1994. I could tell by looking at my little brother that something was wrong. The robust young boxer I had seen before was gone, replaced by a man who looked too tired and empty to be Leon.

"Don't tell me you're dying," I blurted out before he could say a word. "Man, please don't tell me it's HIV and AIDS." I had never talked to Leon about his sexuality and it didn't matter to me. But while working as a porter in the hospital I had seen the suffering that victims of this cruel disease endured; I was the guy who packed up the clothes of the dead in the basement. This was before there was anything doctors could do to slow the disease down or give a patient any hope of surviving. Now Leon nodded his head, and Allen Thomas started to cry.

"Goddamn," I swore to a God I now worshipped but could not fathom. "Another fucking brother, man?" I turned to Leon, wishing there was some way to fight this fight for him, to be the big brother who could step in and save him. I said the only thing left for me to say.

"Yo, man, you know I love you, man."

I got to see him one more time after that, before being called to the chaplain's office.

I rode to Leon's funeral shackled in a prison van with two officers to guard me. Traffic was terrible, and the CO driving—Murphy was his name, and we knew each other because he managed boxers on the outside—got lost on the way to Brooklyn. It took us five hours to make what should have been a ninety-minute trip at the most. When we finally got there, we walked in, and the pastor was the only one there.

"You missed it," he said.

The COs went into damage control. "Yo, man, don't get us in trouble," they implored me. "Don't say anything."

I was quiet. Maybe it just wasn't meant for me to see my little brother in a coffin. Maybe this wasn't God punishing me, but God sparing me just that one piece of pain.

Back in the van, my silence made the COs anxious.

"Yo, man, why ain't you crying?" one of them asked.

"For what?" I answered dully. "This is the way my life has been. Just like this."

Murphy said he wished he had a fighter like me, then asked if there was something they could do to make this any better.

"Get me some street food," I suggested.

They pulled up to some joint and bought a bag of burgers, then loosened my handcuffs so I could eat. Back at Sing Sing, I never said a word about missing my brother's funeral. It was just the way my life was, that's all.

7

AS THE YEARS SLOWLY PASSED, and I became more educated and more spiritual, a new restlessness set in. I became less resigned to the solitary confinement my heart was serving. My boxing, plus the classes and workshops I continually signed up for, had given me regular contact with good, compassionate people from the outside, and I was beginning to realize that, contrary to what I'd heard all my life, maybe I wasn't worthless. Knowing that I had the ability to contribute positively to society made me eager to give something of myself. I know that sounds high-minded and maybe even insincere. But my whole life had been about survival, about resorting, even as a kid, to taking what I needed because I knew I couldn't count on anyone else to provide for me. I pretty much raised myself, and I can tell you right now that a child who's forced to do that is bound to grow up selfish and distrustful. Shariff and the Muslim lifers who mentored me saw right through that childish posturing, though, and the true gift they gave me, through prayer and meditation, was self-awareness. I'll always be grateful to them for that. The world does work in mysterious ways, and ultimately, it was these supposedly stone-cold criminals who set me right. My faith before had been shallow and easily abandoned in the face of injustice. Believing in God again—truly believing and trusting in his plan—allowed me to believe in myself. It doesn't get any simpler.

Religion is a subject that came to fascinate me. Whether I was reading the Qu'ran or the Bible, or studying Asian philosophy and the ancient martial arts, I was drawn to the idea of being an honorable man—one who provided for and protected his wife and children and humbly served his community. I liked to picture myself in a business suit someday, coming home from work to a house full of kids and the smell of dinner on the stove. I would be married to a good woman, and we would live in our own house, drive a nice car, save enough to send our children to college. I would fill my shelves with as many books and CDs as I wanted without anyone telling me what I was or wasn't allowed to enjoy. I would wear whatever color clothes I pleased, and good shoes. In my free time, I would introduce at-risk kids to boxing, returning the favor the great Floyd Patterson and Bob Jackson once did for me. Maybe I could shape the promising ones into real contenders. It would feel good to at least give some other young man the chance that had been taken away from me. I would be surrounded by people I cared about, and who cared about me in return.

That was my fantasy. My reality was that none of the families waiting in line on visiting day belonged to me, and my name was not going to be called to walk through that orange door unless my lawyers had business to discuss. The rare visits I got weren't nearly enough to sustain me, so I had to get creative. Eventually I found my own way to be around the visiting-day families: I became their photographer.

After I completed the photographer's training and got the

job through the Jaycee program, I became a fixture in Sing Sing's visiting room, taking family portraits for my fellow inmates. The big room was bursting with the conflicting emotions of so many people torn apart by crime. Working that room, I would see the tears rolling down the cheeks of bone-tired mothers who left packages of cookies and cigarettes for the sons who had been swept up by the streets and landed in prison. I'd watch the little kids light up under the attention of daddies they barely knew, while the older kids tried to hide the pain they felt inside with long silences and blank stares. I saw the prison groupie girlfriends servicing their con-artist cons, going as far as they possibly could before a CO spotted them and broke it up. In that room, all kinds of promises would be made and broken. Sometimes family ties would tighten, and sometimes they would snap. Sometimes marriages held strong as cement, and sometimes you could watch them crumble before your eyes. In the visiting room, people had no choice but to say whatever they had to say for anyone to hear, whether they were voicing their loyalty or their doubts, their love or their contempt. Sometimes the smiles my camera captured were real, but a lot of times, it seemed, they were just a masquerade. It's funny how you get a feel for what's genuine or not by looking through that little lens.

Prison rules banned female visitors from wearing provocative clothing, like see-through blouses or tight pants, but that didn't stop some women from pushing the boundaries. You could still get an eyeful when you scanned the room; plenty of the women were all but screaming for attention. They didn't get mine: it was the composed, understated women who piqued my interest. One day—this was in the springtime of 1995—an inmate's sister came to visit, and I went up to take a picture. "Hey, this is Sing Sing's light-heavyweight champion," the inmate, Joseph, said by way of introduction.

Trena possessed that kind of quiet demeanor that speaks volumes. She carried herself like a woman, not a little girl. You could see the intelligence sparkling in her brown eyes and feel the warmth in her pretty smile. I was happily surprised when Trena told me how much she loved boxing; she had grown up watching it with her dad. We stood there talking for a good twenty minutes. Trena was twenty-eight, about seven years younger than I was. She had been going to college to become a teacher, majoring in psychology so she could work with special needs kids, but her financial aid had run out one semester short of graduation, and she was working then for a discount stock brokerage firm. She was a single mom with a daughter named Diamond, who was just three. She and the baby's father had just split up, and he put them out of the house. She was on the verge of becoming homeless and landing in a family shelter with Diamond when her sickly father came to the rescue and suggested they rent a two-bedroom place together.

I wanted to meet her ex in the boxing ring, right then and there, for a little tune-up. I've never been able to abide men who treat women badly. The sick feeling it gives me probably goes back to the way Dirty Harry used my mother as his speed bag when I was a helpless little kid. Even when I took to the streets as a teen and ran with a rough crowd, I couldn't act the role of macho gangster that other dudes did, slapping their girlfriends around, expecting them to obey commands like some dog, and calling them all bitches, or worse. At Sing Sing, there were guys who would curse their own mothers out in the visiting room: *Didn't I fucking tell you to bring me Snickers?* Some guys would manipulate a whole string of groupie pen pals or whoever else they could bait and hook, staggering the visiting days so each one thought she was the only "fiancée" bringing packages, putting money in a con's commissary account, and giving a quick hand job under the table when the CO wasn't looking. These were the same dudes who expected their women to smuggle in cash or contraband. Some of them, foolish enough to bring in drugs, were caught and ended up behind bars themselves. You think the inmate who put them up to it felt even a little bit sorry? Hell, no. He just moved on to Bachelorette number 2 . . . or number 22. It was as predictable as the plot of Dick and Jane, except, when it got to the critical part, Jane didn't have the sense to run. You'd walk into the room, see a guy all buffed up—good physique, handsome—sitting there with a girl five foot four, hundred and eighty pounds, wearing her desperation like cheap perfume, and you'd think, *Here it goes again*. She would be the only one in the room who didn't know he was flat-out using her.

Being the detached observer in that room a couple of days a week was like an advanced course in psychology. You would see the way a rapist behaved around a woman, how his cowardly need to dominate and hurt seemed to be always simmering just below the surface. You'd see how some men laid their wives or girlfriends out when the CO wasn't looking, because they didn't bring what they wanted. *Yo, bitch, where my money at?* You see him take a swing at her, you don't tell the COs, because they could shut down visiting day right then and there for everybody. There were better ways to deal with that kind of disrespect. My status as a prison boxer had given me some credibility as a private peacekeeper, so if I saw some dude pulling that kind of shit, I would wait until I could get him on the other side of the orange door to get in his face: "What the fuck is *wrong* with you, man?" is usually all it took.

The funny thing is, Trena told me much later that she had had a strong jolt of intuition about me before we even met that first time. She vividly remembers some inner voice speaking to her as she and her brother came up to get their picture taken. *This man is going to be prosperous one day* is what she heard. Once I'd taken their shot, I asked Trena if she minded if I took a picture of just her.

"No, I don't mind," she said. I snapped the Polaroid, then took the picture, and put it in my pocket. It was my way of saying I was interested.

I'd never met someone like Trena before, who could just dive right into the deep end of a conversation. We talked about the passion we both had for education, and the role of faith in our lives. It felt so good to have a stimulating conversation that had nothing to do with Sing Sing and the hell kept hidden behind that orange door. It felt indescribably good just to click with someone, and not have to plow through all that superficial bullshit you usually do when you're sizing somebody up to see where the person fits in your life. I told her in our very first conversation that I was innocent, in jail for a crime I didn't commit. I didn't share the details, but I talked my head off. When it was time for her to leave, I cut straight to the chase. I was nowhere near as smooth as I thought I was.

"You need to know that I'm not looking for a friend. I'm looking for a wife," I informed Trena. New York had changed its mind about letting lifers marry and had lifted its ban in 1990. Working the visiting room gave me the possibility of actually meeting somebody and marrying someday, of having somebody who would help me do my time. My ideal woman would be someone who was smart and had a strong backbone; I didn't want some meek little mouse who just said yes, yes, yes all the time with no convictions of her own. Independence was high on my list of desirable traits, and I also knew I wanted someone as interested in pursuing her education as I was in continuing mine. I'd chatted up women before during my roving photographer gig—always making sure it wasn't someone's wife or girlfriend—but Trena was the first one I considered a serious prospect.

And now she was looking at me like I was crazy.

Trena's response to my forthright declaration about finding a wife sent me backpedaling for some dignity fast. I decided education was a safer topic, and I heard myself urging her to go back and finish her degree so she could build a better life for herself and her daughter. Still trying to cover my embarrassment, I told her she should also be in touch with God on a daily basis. Trena listened politely and, to her everlasting credit, did not cut me down then and there, though she later admitted to bursting out in laughter once she got to the parking lot, thinking it took one helluva nerve for a guy serving twenty years to life in prison to play like he was some damn life coach. *Handsome but cocky* is how she summed me up back then. And she had no intention of becoming some jailbird's bride, thank you just the same. It's safe to say that Sing Sing was not her matchmaker of choice.

By the time she got home, I had already called and chatted up her father for half an hour.

"Dewey wants to know if you'd be interested in coming to some festival at Sing Sing," Trena's dad helpfully relayed. Trena was surprised and not very pleased that her brother had given up her phone number to some felon she had just met, but my intentions were purely honorable. The Muslims were hosting a big festival in the prison gym, very family oriented, and we needed to sign up our guests well in advance so they could be cleared for the special visiting privilege. As best as you could when locked up in prison, I was asking Trena out on a date.

It was another week before I got another turn at the phone and was able to call her again. The long wait worked in my favor, though, and whatever initial hesitation Trena felt had given way to an oh-why-not curiosity. She accepted my invitation.

On the day of the festival, I dressed up as much as the prison rulebook would allow me, pulling on my best green sweater over a crisp white shirt I had arranged to have cleaned and pressed by an associate who worked in the laundry. Trena arrived in a nice dress, looking every inch the lady. I felt nervous, but she quickly put me at ease. We enjoyed the food, music, and all the kids happily racing around getting their faces painted and playing the little games that had been set up for them. She stayed for hours, until the festival ended around two thirty in the afternoon. We talked all day, but the conversation that stuck with me most was the one we had about family. She casually asked me if I had any siblings.

"Yeah, I got sisters and brothers all over the place," I said, shrugging. "But nobody sees after me." In time, she would learn what had happened to them, and to me.

Trena took my hand.

"Well, guess what," she said. "I'll be your family."

Who asked who for that first kiss is a matter of ongoing dispute, but I do remember chiding her for being too prim.

"Why you giving me a white-girl kiss?" I objected. "I want a real kiss!"

"Wow, you're pretty straightforward," she checked me, even as she obliged.

We began writing letters back and forth, several times a week, and Trena would let me know when she was coming to visit her brother. She often brought his young daughter to see him, and while the two of them were visiting, Trena would slip away and come hang out with me. My method of courting outside of prison had always amounted to this: sit down at a bar, go home with a woman. Either she would lie down and have sex with you, or not. You didn't have to prove yourself.

Now I understood that I had to be appealing and respectful. Most important of all, I wanted Trena to see that my word was good. I resolved to be attentive to everything she said and did, to show her how much I cared however I could. I wasn't in a place where you could buy a nice bouquet and show up with flowers for your sweetheart. But creative people get put in prison, too, and with the right connections, I could buy a beautiful handcrafted greeting card from more than one talented artist doing time, with a message inscribed by my choice of prison poets. If I saved enough forbidden cash or had something worth trading, I could even get Trena a pocketbook from a guy who did designer-quality custom leatherwork from his cell.

After a while, Trena got on my visiting list and began coming specifically to see me, which caused some tension between me and her brother, who felt cheated out of his own visits and worried that Trena would spend what little money she had on packages for me instead of him. Sing Sing allowed visitors every day during the week, and alternating weekends. Trena lived in Beacon, which was just fifteen or twenty minutes up the Hudson River. She began coming to see me sometimes twice, three times a week. That told me a lot. I never asked her for anything, but I was grateful for the snacks she would buy us from the vending machines only the visitors were allowed to use. We would picnic on Big Az cheese-burgers and hot wings that Trena would nuke in the visiting room microwave. There was watery orange Tang to drink and candy bars for dessert—I had given up smoking without much trouble, but I craved sweets like crazy. We'd spend our time talking and laughing together, or sometimes we'd just sit holding hands, enjoying what little physical contact was allowed. I loved the way she would sometimes lay her head on my shoulder.

The first time Trena brought Diamond to meet me, we were just sitting down at our assigned table when I saw two guys out of the corner of my eye getting ready to fight. There was no shouting, no commotion, or anything yet, but in that split second, I knew it was going to go down. I jumped up without a word and pushed Trena—with Diamond still in her arms—behind me. Then I pulled the chairs beside me and the table in front of us.

"If you come over here, I'm gonna bust both your nigger asses," I bellowed at the two men now locked in a brawl. Trena and Diamond both stared at me wide-eyed. Diamond was just a tiny thing, pretty and precious as the gemstone she was named for.

"Why were they fighting?" Trena wondered after COs broke it up.

"I don't know. All I care about is protecting you two," I replied. I knew it was the truest thing I'd ever said the moment the words left my mouth. Protecting them was what I wanted to do for the rest of their lives.

I was a fool for Diamond, but she took her sweet time to warm up to me. She had had her mama to herself for as long as a three-year-old can remember, and she was mad that I was trying to horn in on her territory. At first, she refused to come to me or let on that she was interested in any of the toys I showed her in the little play area set aside for prisoners' kids. But once she decided I passed muster, she would reach out her little arms to greet me whenever she saw me and then spend most of our visit sitting on top of my shoulders. We'd color pictures together, and I tried to teach her numbers. She loved going down the little plastic slide in the play area.

Trena never missed a visit. It made my day when I knew she was coming. I would shower, then go to my cell and read a little for school until it was time to go down. Visiting hours were nine in the morning until three in the afternoon.

Trena was becoming part of my world. I wasn't sure she understood what that meant, at first: my world was a prison. I never forgot that, much as I tried to pretend otherwise when we were together. I couldn't always pull it off. One time, just as I was about to clear all the checkpoints and go into the visiting room for my shift as photographer, a newjack decided to throw his weight around and put me through the full cheek-baring routine. The rookie CO could see I was fuming and using every ounce of my willpower not to mouth off at him, so he pushed even harder: he decreed that the shirt I was wearing was in violation of the dress code somehow. I don't even remember what the problem was—I always wore my nicest clothes when I was going to see Trena, and I knew she was going to be there to see her brother that day. I was ordered to go back to my cell and change.

Clothes were an easy way to jam everything up for an inmate on visiting days. Some of the female COs made it practically a team sport to harass the girlfriends or wives passing through security on the other side, turning them back because their pants were too tight or their blouses too sheer, or the bras they were wearing had hooks that set off the metal detector. The meaner COs took sadistic pleasure in fucking up your day, maybe even your relationship if they pushed hard enough. ("I don't wanna visit you anyways. That bitch made me change twice!") I wasn't going to give up that easy, though. The trip to my cell and back just to put on a different shirt, plus the whole hassle of waiting in line and passing through security again, was going to cost me an hour of precious time at the least. If I made a big scene over it, I could get written up for disobeying a direct order and end up in keep-lock. I hurried back as fast as I could, but the whole episode left me agitated, and once I finally got through that orange door, I was in a dark-cloud mood. I spotted Trena but didn't go up to greet her. Instead, I bustled around taking my pictures, all business, avoiding the anxious glances she was shooting my way. When she finally sought me out and gave me a hug, I was still in my mood, and barely acknowledged her. I could see she was upset and confused by the brush-off. I didn't understand why I was pushing her away, either, just when our friendship was on the verge of becoming something more. I felt like a jerk. I caught her on her way out the door, bent down, and whispered in her ear.

"I love you."

She smiled, and I knew all had been forgiven.

Once I fell in love, I felt like a man split into two. When I came into that visiting room, I could let go a little, and just breathe. I was nice. I was funny. I was positive and upbeat. I was the very best version I had of myself. But the minute I got on the other side of that door, it was like I had just passed through the gates of hell and knew full well what misery was awaiting me. I had to change into someone else. On that side of the door, I had to carry myself differently. I had to come off like a cold, vicious person, like someone you wouldn't ever want to mess with, because the only way to make sure you didn't get stabbed, beat down, or jumped on was to instill fear in anyone who might try. That was a possibility I had to deal with every single day. You had to be a rattlesnake always coiled to strike. There were so many times when I woke up angry and frustrated, but Trena would be visiting later in the day, and it would take every ounce of energy and willpower I had to summon forth my best self again for those few treasured hours that I'd be able to spend with the caramel-skinned woman and sweet baby girl I now considered my family.

We hit our first serious bump in the road a few months into our relationship when I felt like the time had come to explain my case to her. I had told her at the outset how much time I was doing, but I hadn't said why or laid out the specifics. I didn't know that she had asked her brother to ask around about me already, or that he had reported back to her that I had been convicted of murdering an old woman. That Trena didn't judge me should tell you a lot about her character and her Christianity. On the day I decided it was time to share my whole story, I felt excited as I put all my news clippings and some of my legal casework into a fresh new file folder for her. I wanted her to understand what I was going through and what I was fighting for. And yes, I wanted her to do what she could do to help me, to feel outraged by what had happened and join my fight. It wasn't Trena's money I wanted. It was her devotion. I wanted her to make phone calls, to make contact with whatever potentially useful organizations or individuals she could reach more easily than I could. Most of all, I wanted to know she believed me.

Trena pushed the file back across the table. She wanted no part of it.

To her, our relationship existed separately from my legal dilemma. She knew I was doing twenty to life and wouldn't even come up for parole for the first time for another eight years, that I was trying to prove my innocence in the meantime, but she considered all that a matter best handled by me, God, and the State of New York. She didn't want to deal with my past. Her lack of interest stung, and I wasn't sure what to make of it. Did she think deep down that I might be guilty? I was too scared to ask her point-blank. And if that were the case, why would she even want to be around me? There is a whole raft of control-freak women out there who actually *prefer* men in prison just so they can call all the shots, and never have to deal with the complicated business of living to-gether, but Trena did not fit that bill at all. I was baffled. I took back my folder and tried to convince myself that it was just too soon, and I had overwhelmed her. We didn't mention it again. I prayed that the day would come when she would ask to see it.

TRENA AND I HAD KNOWN EACH OTHER JUST SHY OF A YEAR when I leaned in close during one of our visits and whispered in her ear: "Would you marry me?"

Trena pulled back and looked at me like I was crazy.

"I have to think about that," she said carefully.

The next two weeks were agony for me. I knew Trena cared about me, but my sentence was twenty years to life. To life. There was a possibility that I would never walk out the gates of Sing Sing, that I would die behind bars. Trena's brother, serving his own fifteen-year sentence a few cells down from me, urged her not to become a prisoner's wife. "Yo, I heard him on the phone with her," a friend of mine reported. "He was saying don't do it."

Trena continued to write and visit me while she was mulling over my proposal, and when I saw her again, I tried to bolster my case.

"I know what your brother is saying, and I understand," I ar-gued. "I wouldn't want this for my sister, either. But I love you. I know I can't prove who I am as a man in here, but if God lets me out, I'll show you. I'll take care of you."

Trena had girlfriends whose men had been locked up then got out, and she knew that there was no such thing as a storybook ending. Being released from prison doesn't necessarily mean you are freed from prison. Prison can follow you into the real world, box you in mentally just as surely as it did physically.

"All you guys say that crap," Trena challenged me, "and then you walk out and treat your women like dirt."

"But I'm not them," I insisted.

"I don't know that, Dewey."

"That's why you gotta trust me."

The next time I wrote her, I asked her to go buy a certain tape by Babyface, one of my favorite artists. "Please listen to all those songs," I implored her. Even the titles—"Given a Chance," "Sunshine," and "I'll Give the World to You"—had special meaning to me. Trena did as I asked.

"Why did you tell me to listen to those songs?" she wanted to know the next visiting day.

"Because that's me," I said. "That's me talking to you."

Trena fell quiet.

"Are you sure this is what you want?" she finally asked.

"No," I corrected her, "are you sure this is what you can do?"

"The only way I'll marry you is if you ask my dad," Trena said. She was a grown woman of nearly thirty, with a child of her own, but Trena had an old-school way to her that I found not only charming, but reassuring. The way she stuck by her jailed brother and looked after her ailing father proved to me that when Trena made a commitment, she stood by it. Now she wanted to do everything properly, and if having me ask her father for her hand in marriage was important to her, then it was important to me. She brought him with her the next time she came. We had spoken on the phone before, talked sports and such, but I had never seen him face-to-face. He was a serious, older gentleman who knew what was coming. He was friendly but reserved, and I could tell he was sizing me up—how I dressed and how I was groomed, how I carried myself, how I sounded.

"Listen," I began, hoping I didn't sound as nervous as I felt. "I was wondering if you would mind if I asked for your daughter's hand in marriage." What else could I say? I had nothing else to offer. I couldn't promise a beautiful life.

"No, I don't mind," he answered. "Just make sure you take care of her. Be a man of your word."

"That's not something you have to worry about," I vowed. Trena came back, and I kissed her before walking away. It was all pretty awkward, but nothing had ever felt so right in my life.

We put in the paperwork to get married, and we were assigned a date a few months down the road: March 30, 1996.

Sing Sing held weddings in the main building, in what had been the original visiting room. There was nothing romantic about it—it was just another dingy room to shuffle inmates into and out of. We were married by the prison chaplain, with two friends from the outside and COs serving as witnesses. Trena wore a beige dress and held Diamond in her arms. I wore my state-issued best. Trena bought us both rings—the first of three I would end up going through in the course of our marriage thanks to a strong left jab I have on the heavy punching bag.

We had to wait a year for our honeymoon.

Sing Sing had six trailers for conjugal visits, parked side by side in a sort of makeshift campground on an isolated patch of land up a little hill from the cellblocks. Each trailer had a little kitchen, a living room, a bathroom, and two bedrooms—one for a child, the other for the parents. You had to show a CO all the knives, forks, and spoons before you left. If you broke anything, you had to report it. In prison, a shard of glass can become deadly. Homemade shivs and spears could be buried in the recreation yard or the old baseball field. When the COs found out, the prison tore up all the grass and made it hardscape from then on.

Our honeymoon was two days in one of the trailers. It had been so long since I had been with a woman, years upon years. *Damn, is this really going to happen?* I thought as I helped Trena put away the lasagna she had made—my favorite dish. I ate as much as my stomach could hold, relishing every rich bite. Just being able to open a refrigerator door and help myself—to have a soda or orange juice when I wanted to—was more gratifying than you would ever expect such an ordinary thing to be. Just being in the little trailer with this beautiful woman who was now my wife—my *wife*—felt shocking to me. During our courtship in the visiting room, I would walk right up to Trena and give her a kiss. But here, I felt strange. Cuddling with Trena on the sofa, all my boldness was gone, replaced by a shyness I'd never experienced before. She finally made a move on me, and we made our way into the bedroom. Our first time together as husband and wife was full of unspoken emotion, compassionate and tender.

I couldn't stay in bed, though. As night fell, I started hearing noises. I didn't feel comfortable being in the trailer. It wasn't like a cell, locked tight at night, with bars you could see through to know if someone was approaching. The trailer felt exposed and vulnerable. Anyone could get in, sneak up on you. The darkness was darker than the cellblock, the silence deeper. Every sound made me jump. The knives in the kitchen were attached to the wall with a wire, but I grabbed one and put it on the table, as close to the door as it would reach. I had to defend my family. I didn't trust anybody, not even the COs.

"Dewey, what's wrong?" Trena whispered. I paced back and forth to the dirty little window, peering out. Adrenaline pulsed through my body as if I were about to step into the ring, and my subconscious put me through the same mental paces it did during a fight: *Keep moving, keep moving, don't let your guard down, anticipate, anticipate.* I sat and stared at the door, listening and waiting. I couldn't sleep in the soft bed, anyway, after a decade on the hard iron bed in my cell. I wished I could sleep on the floor. The refrigerator thumped, and I was up like a shot, convinced someone was in the living room.

It was then that I knew just how institutionalized I had become, and how deeply prison had wounded me. I realized that Trena was the only person left in the world I trusted. I held her tight, and when daylight came, I was able to pretend again that everything was all right.

8

HUMANITY CANNOT EXIST WITHOUT HOPE, and there is nothing sadder than watching a man lose both.

In prison, a soul can get scraped away methodically, like a piece of metal sharpened against a concrete cell floor night after night. Other times, it happens in a shocked instant, like a force of nature, the way a tornado strips the bark right off a tree then leaves it standing, leafless and raw. I knew the day I callously stepped over the bleeding body of that inmate who had just been stabbed that my humanity had deserted me. I remember just as vividly the day it returned.

There was a guy on my cellblock who had given up. The guy just stayed in his cell all the time. He never came out to shower or to get some fresh air in the yard. After a while, he began to smell, the stink of sickness and surrender coming off him so bad that people started complaining about having to even walk past his cell. The other inmates shunned him like a leper, and even the COs kept their distance. He was like some pathetic animal that had crawled off to just wait for death to hurry up and come. His cell looked like an overturned Dumpster, filled with trash and God only knows what. One day when I was hurrying past, trying not to breathe, I saw him stir in his cot, and the pity rose up and hit me out of nowhere. The loneliness and cruelty of his situation made me stop in my tracks and call out to him.

"How you doing?" I asked. "Can I talk to you a minute?" He came up to the bars.

"Yo, I don't want to be rude, but can I ask you something?"

He nodded.

"Why you don't care for yourself anymore? Why you let yourself go like that? Why you live like this?" I wanted to know.

He opened up his shirt so I could see the purple marks on his skin, telling me without a word that life didn't mean anything anymore.

Damn, I thought. *AIDS*. His misery was ten times, a hundred times, my own.

"Well, if I was to do something for you, would you be a man and take care of yourself?" I heard myself cajoling him. He looked wary, not sure what to make of me. We didn't even know each other's name.

"No one cares, no one really gives a damn," he countered.

"If I was to offer you a shower, if I was to clean your cell, would you take care of yourself?" I pressed. He studied me for a moment before deciding.

"Yeah."

"Okay, I got you then. Go get ready."

I went to the officers on gallery duty, told them about the deal I had struck, and asked them to give the inmate permission to take a shower and me the go-ahead to clean out his cell while he was gone.

"Really?" the sergeant said, surprised by the prospect of such community service. "Why you want to bother with that mother-fucker?"

"Yo, man, the man is dying, let me help him out."

Permission was instantly granted, and while the man showered, I filled bags with all the trash and carried it out, swept out his cell, then mopped it and swabbed down every surface with Ajax. He came back, and I got permission to get fresh sheets and a clean blanket for his fetid bed, which he made up himself. I went and got his filthy clothes washed. He didn't have a whole lot more time left in this world, and I won't lie and say we became great friends, but as I scrubbed out his cell that day, I felt something I had been missing for a good long time: I felt connected, by however fragile a thread, to another human being.

A couple of mornings later, his cell was empty. I don't know whether he died or was finally sent to the hospital, or if something else happened.

I never did know his name.

CRIMINALS WEREN'T THE ONLY ONES TO LOSE THEIR SOULS IN SING SING. There were COs every bit as inhuman as the worst baby killers and rapists in the place. One officer was known for ordering inmates down on the ground during cell searches so he could accidentally grind his boot down on a man's hand until the bones crunched. Applause broke out when news traveled through the galleries that he had died in a car crash one weekend while off duty.

One of the worst incidents happened when a sadistic sergeant named Ronald Hunlock discovered a litter of kittens in a box an inmate had hidden in his cell. Like many prisons, Sing Sing had a colony of stray cats roaming the grounds; their presence was tolerated because they were cheap exterminators when it came to trying to control the vermin. Some animal-loving inmates tamed the wild cats to keep as pets, and most COs just looked the other way. On this particular afternoon, though, Hunlock ordered the inmate to take his box of kittens outside and dump them in the prison trash compactor.

"I'm not going to do that," the prisoner repeatedly said.

Hunlock then grabbed the box, threw the five kittens into the compactor himself, and flipped the switch.

The inmate reported him, and the officer was convicted of animal cruelty, fired, and sentenced to a year in jail. He was lucky to have faced justice in the courtroom instead of the cellblocks.

Inmates live by their own code of conduct even in a maximum-security facility like Sing Sing. In one year alone in the early 1980s, there were twenty-one stabbings at Sing Sing—two of them fatal—and weapons seized included homemade icepicks, a kitchen ladle, and a fifteen-inch knife. You could rip a piece of metal off an old radiator, sharpen it, put tape around it for a handle, and you had a shank. There were even armed robberies inside prison—a jewel thief I knew who served as the banker for an inside gambling operation got stabbed in the chest with a 007 switchblade by inmates in ski masks who ransacked his cell in search of the hidden cash. Some other guys and I walked in right after and found him bleeding on the floor. We grabbed one of the stretchers out on the galleries and ran him down to the hospital on the first floor. He survived and was transferred to another prison.

The yard was segregated by tacit inmate agreement. The Bloods had their section over by the heavy bag where I did my workouts.

The Crips eyed them with menace from their own territory across the yard. The Muslims, Jamaicans, Latin Kings, and Aryan Brothers claimed their real estate, as well. I stayed neutral.

The mood could change in a blue-sky moment. Shit happened so fast. A kid with "white" tattooed on one arm and "power" on the other is suddenly screaming in line, blood pouring from the slash marks that will scar his face for life: *Yo, yo, yo, why'd you do that to me?* And nobody saying a word until out in the yard a brother laughs. *Well, now you got a reason to hate us.*

Out in the yard, you would feel the tension, low and heavy as a ground fog, then everything would explode. All you could do was just try to get out of the way and watch. My instincts were good enough and my feet fast enough that I usually made it, but one time I had the bad luck of being smack in the middle of it. I had been standing with the Muslims when a Blood came up and reached up without a word to slice open this Muslim's face.

"Get him!" I heard someone shout, and then all hell broke loose. People were getting bashed with weights, stabbed, beaten with sticks that had nails stuck in them, stomped. A guard in the tower popped off a shot. Officers were screaming at everyone to get down on the ground. I was fighting with some guy when I heard a CO yell at me: "Get down on the floor, Bozella!"

"Hell, no!" I shouted back. I wasn't about to lie down in a full-out riot. "I'll go to the fence," I countered. The CO could have had me then and there for disobeying a direct order, but he waved me away. I loved him for that. Martinez, I remember his name. As I got up, he called out to me.

"You know why I let you go, Bozella?" I looked at him and shook my head.

"Because I know you don't mess with nobody."

I had years of good behavior behind me by then. I was the very definition of model prisoner. The CO knew that if I was fighting, the dude I laid out had to have done something very, very wrong. It was as strange a place as any to get some validation, in the middle of a prison riot, but I have to admit that I felt gratified.

Another time, we were in the chapel watching a movie, back when they had reel-to-reels in the '80s. A young brother, a Muslim, got into a fight, and I dragged him outside to break it up. A CO was on him as well and had a baton to his throat. I grabbed the stick because it was choking him out. I was getting ready to pick him up and throw him over my shoulder, get him away from there. Another officer then put a stick on me. I could see everybody coming out of the theater. The mood was ugly. It was going to be out-and-out inmates versus officers.

"Don't put the stick on me, man," I warned the officer. "Look!"

He glanced behind himself and saw the inmates gathering into a single angry knot. He took the stick off me. I raised my arms to stop the agitated crowd. "It's aight," I called out, "everything's aight." Everybody went back inside to watch the movie, and I got keep-lock for thirty days. One of the officers spoke up on my behalf before the Adjustment Committee: "If not for him," he said, "we'd have had an all-out riot." I was offered a transfer to a medium-security facility as a sort of reward, I guess, but I turned it down. I liked being around serious people, not kids. Sing Sing was a better spot to get my life together.

The chapel uprising was nothing compared to a personal test I faced in that same place right after my second conviction. I had come down to find some peace one morning, and when I went inside, there was Stanley Jackson. *Aw shit,* I swore to myself, *how in the hell am I supposed to deal with this? Are we gonna have to fight?*

Half the people inside the chapel knew this was the guy who had killed my brother Ernie, and I could feel everyone watching me. I looked at him, didn't say a word, and got the hell out the first chance I had, the past flashing in front of me all the way back to my cell. I wanted to rip his head off. The galleries started to crackle with excitement and blood lust. Everyone assumed that I would come for Stanley Jackson. And it's true: I had wanted to kill him for years to avenge Ernie's murder. I used to fantasize about beating the life right out of Stanley Jackson. With my opportunity finally at hand, all the old hurt came back to me.

The code of the street is: *Go get him, get even, you better leave him with a mark.* Prison code is: *Yo, man, we know that nigger did your brother; hit him upside the head with a metal pipe, stab him with a 007 knife or shank, there's a job for you to do. We waitin'.* If you did nothing, you would be marked yourself: punk, coward, pussy, sissy, faggot, all the things not a man.

Three days later, I was going to school one afternoon, and there was Stanley out on the flats. But here's the catch: You got three tiers above the flats with guys looking down because they knew all hell was about to break loose. They were waiting for a show. The pressure's on me to deliver. I'm not trying to say Stanley's a punk. He was going to fight back. The only question was: *Do I want to live by prison code, or be my own man and say, let this shit go, live my own life?* I walked up to Stanley and planted myself in front of him. I could feel a hundred eyes watching.

"First, I just want to know one thing," I said. "Why? Why did you murder my brother?"

Stanley Jackson shrugged.

"I was young," he replied.

I did the unthinkable, then. I hugged my brother's killer.

"I forgive you," I said, then walked away.

Even my closest allies were infuriated. An inmate imam up-braided me at services. *That was your brother! Your brother!*

"Yo," I answered back with measured respect. "That's between me and my God. It's got nothing to do with anyone else."

Fuck the prison code. Fuck the code of the street. That was the birth of my true identity. That was my true test as a man and human being. I wanted to move on with my life. I had to forgive if I wanted to be fucking forgiven.

9

WHENEVER IT CAME OUR TURN FOR A CONJUGAL VISIT AT THE TRAILERS—once every three or four months—Trena and I seized the chance to pretend for a fleeting weekend that we were just like any married couple, settled and comfortable in our life together. It was a play in one act, based on the shared fantasy we both needed to believe in to escape the harsh realities we each faced when it was time to return to our separate worlds. Trena packed comfortable clothes for me to change into and arrived with bags of permitted groceries, including the prison-inspected ingredients for her homemade lasagna. Everything had to come into Sing Sing factory sealed. That they were so worried about what contraband might slip into Sing Sing in a casserole was pretty laughable, considering that drug operations were already flourishing in the cellblocks. Trena never complained about the searches, and her pleasant demeanor bought her some slack from the guards, which gave her the chance to sneak in her cell phone to stay in touch with Diamond. Bustling about in that tiny trailer kitchen, fixing supper for her husband, Trena had a softness to her that allowed me to believe we would be the exception to the accepted wisdom that prison marriages never last. It's not so much that these marriages crumble under the stress; it's more that they never have a chance to grow in the first place. Relationships get boxed in, trapped by the routine and restrictions, with no space to flourish. You can't learn the intricate footwork of your dance together—you can't squabble over household chores, or tease each other out of a bad mood, or debate what kind of car to buy, or even talk about the movie you just saw together. You can sign the piece of paper legally declaring you husband and wife and you can wear your rings, but at the end of the day, you're forced to live your separate lives, and your marriage exists mostly in your mind. I had seen the way most prison wives would come through the visiting room, wearing their resentment or resignation like their jeans, so tight they could barely breathe. In the cozy cocoon of our trailer, I convinced myself that Trena and I were smart enough and devoted enough to hold on until I won my freedom. Music playing, pots clanging, the smell of lasagna wafting from the kitchen—I felt the worry unhitch from my mind and gorged myself into a contented stupor on Trena's cooking and conversation, settling into the temporary rhythm of what I imagined an ordinary life to be. For two days, we would make love and talk and fall asleep in each other's arms without the sharp command of visiting room guards forbidding us to touch or kiss or hug too close or too long. I could wake up in the middle of the night and raid the refrigerator for leftovers when I was hungry, or pour myself a glass of orange juice when I was thirsty, drinking as much as I wanted. I could turn the lights on or off when I felt like it, or stay in the shower until the hot water ran out. I could hear silence again, feel it sweep through my mind like a stream, crystal clean.

Three times a day, the phone would ring to make sure I hadn't escaped. I was expected to answer with my name and rattle off my prison ID number. One time, Trena grabbed the phone before I could get it. She lowered her voice as deep as it would go: "Bozella, 84A0172," she barked, hanging up just in time before the two of us busted out laughing. The CO on the other end was either the weakest link in Sing Sing's security system, or smart enough to know that there was no way I ever would have even considered bolting and leaving Trena behind. The state had its definition of maximum security, and I finally had mine.

We both dreaded saying good-bye. Trena would try to detach gradually, busying herself by packing up everything to go, and I would change back into my inmate clothes. But we never really bought our own nonchalant act, and we always wound up snuggling together in a chair by the door, listening to "Sunshine," the Babyface track I had claimed as our song after the first time we met. The phone would ring again. "It's time," the bored guard on the other end would say. Watching Trena head for the parking lot while I walked back to the cellblocks was harder than just walking back to the gallery on a regular visiting day. This felt more like saying good-bye to the life I was supposed to have, the one that was unjustly taken from me. Every time she left, I wondered how many years more we would have to live like this. On the day Trena married me, my first parole hearing was still eight years away, and there was no guarantee the board would grant my release. Ever. Twenty years to life, I didn't need to remind myself. *To life.*

I knew Trena was struggling to scrape together a decent life for herself and Diamond on the outside, and it hurt not to be able to take care of them the way I wanted to. I had an old-school idea of how a man should be: I wanted to be the benevolent ruler of my kingdom, the strong but loving provider who fulfilled his family's every need and shielded them from any possible hurt or harm. I'm not trying to pass judgment on anybody, but the truth is, for a sizable majority of the men behind bars, women are just another hustle. I understood why Trena's brother and father had had their reservations until they got to know me. Better to presume a con is shady until he proves otherwise. I wanted to be Trena's benefactor, not her burden. Showing that to her and her family was going to be a challenge, I knew, but I refused to feel helpless and hopeless, no matter how bleak things got. Go down that pity road, and there are no U-turns.

I resolved to do whatever I could for my new family. I wasn't looking to break any laws, but circumventing certain prison rules was another matter, and I approached it the same way I did boxing— you just had to stay focused, anticipate your opponent's moves, and always, always keep moving. The respect and admiration I'd won both as an unbeatable fighter in the ring and a useful peace broker in the prison yard kept the COs at bay long enough for me to conduct my business. My little convenience store had expanded beyond chips and candy bars, and now my cell was more like an underground Walmart neatly hidden beneath my bed. Inmates who were looking to buy new long johns, cigarettes, or a hot chicken dinner were constantly streaming in and out. I started building up an illicit savings account that I buried deep inside my mattress. Trena brought me small gifts I could use for my hustle. The extra socks and sweatsuits she gave me could be flipped into high-ticket items at Sing Sing.

I figured out a way to conceal a couple of twenty-dollar bills in my sneaker without getting detected in a strip-search, and I started sneaking cash to Trena on visiting days. We would sit next to each other and I would stoop down to tie my shoe. *Here,* I'd whisper, swiftly pressing the money into her hand when the guards weren't looking. Luckily, she had a good poker face. She was always grateful, but I knew it wasn't making much of a difference. Even the five or six bucks we used to spend for a vending machine lunch date was a splurge for us: a Big Az cheeseburger for me, a fish sandwich or hot wings for her. Put them in the microwave and it was a Thanksgiving feast. Add a Snickers or Mr. Goodbar for dessert, and it was Christmas.

Once, when she was visiting, Trena mentioned a bus trip her church was taking to North Carolina.

"You wanna go on that trip?" I asked. I could see by the wistful look in her eyes that she did. She shook her head.

"It's a hundred and twenty dollars," she said.

Business was good for me. At one point, I had over fifteen hundred dollars hidden in my mattress. I slipped Trena her bus fare a few bills at a time. She was surprised and grateful. I felt proud that I was showing her that I could take care of her and provide for her, even while I was locked up.

Even in the face of my possible life sentence, Trena held fast to her belief that we would have a good life together someday. Her faith reinforced mine. I would go back to my cell and reread my collection of motivational books and make lists. I had five-year plans. Ten-year plans. Twenty-year plans. From the dog-eared pages of my personal library, Donald Trump, Cus D'Amato, Allah, and Jesus Christ—all urged me on. Education was the constant in my life; what I had squandered on the outside, I hoarded on the inside. In 2000, the Christian Ministry Program helped me enroll in a program to earn a bachelor's degree. I was more naturally inclined to study business, but the program only offered theology, and I thought that was a good fit, too. Hell, it could have been zoology, and I would have jumped at it. I just wanted to be back in school. State and federal budget cutbacks and public resentment over free college educations for convicted felons had pretty much decimated the educational programs in prisons, and I had already earned practically every certificate offered—from prep cook to peer counseling. There wasn't that much left for me to do. Bob Jackson had left the Corrections Department to spend his retirement training fighters at the legendary Gleason's Gym in Brooklyn. I turned my attention instead to martial arts, which I could practice and perfect without attracting much attention. There were inmates who were highly skilled in mixed martial arts—guys who were fourth- and fifth-degree black belts. They knew where the blind alleys were in the galleries and they would hold their secret classes there, the inmate pupils taking turns as lookout. The swiftness and precision the sport demanded was the best survival skill you could have in prison; a single spearlike panther punch to the throat could lay a man flat. It was a thing of beauty to me, and I was equally drawn to the Eastern philosophy behind it that prized self-discipline and respect. I was beyond excited when Trena smuggled in an illustrated 409-page book on Chinese martial arts. It instantly became my most treasured possession. I studied that book like a scholar, practicing each technique until I had it as close to perfect as I could get. My physical training is what kept my mind sharp, and it also kept me motivated. It takes focus and discipline to fine-tune your body, to push through the pain and exhaustion of working each muscle group into compliance, and then, when you think you've achieved peak performance, to raise the bar again and keep working. God tells us that the body is our temple, and I do believe that in my soul, but I also came to understand that the body serves as a teacher, too. Mine was a daily reminder that we have the power to change and to make ourselves stronger or let ourselves grow weaker. We can envision a certain outcome and then work day in and day out to realize it. Whether it was boxing or martial arts, I wanted to be the best. I pictured myself as a champion. *Just practice until you're ready,* I told myself, *and then when you get your chance, fight until you win.*

AS TRENA AND I ADJUSTED TO OUR NEWLYWED LIFE with its regulated routine of authorized visits, censored letters, and brief collect phone calls, Diamond sensed that something had radically changed. I was more than a big playmate she happened to visit now and then over in that noisy place full of men, with vending machines and a toy room. Even as a kindergartner, her territorial instincts were sharp, and within a matter of months, she was pushing me away and howling instead of reaching up to hug me: I was competition as far as she was concerned, and after having Trena to herself her whole life, there was no way Diamond was about to share her mama. Trena didn't force the issue, and I tried my best not to either, much as I yearned to be a father figure to Diamond. There were times that she would run up to me, sit in my lap, and want to snuggle close, but then she would scurry away into her whole separate little world, and it felt like she needed to safeguard her affection. I could see her hurting and understood why she was putting her guard up. One time, when she and Trena were leaving, Diamond stopped and looked back at me with her dark eyes. "When are you getting out of here?" she wanted to know. "I'm working on it," was the best I could tell her. Trena always tried to be honest but vague when Diamond asked about me, but keeping me emotionally present as a part of the family when I wasn't there physically was like trying to put on a puppet show with strings but no dolls. Sometimes Trena folded under the pressure. The worst time was when Diamond was going to appear in a little play at her school. She had badgered Trena, asking whether I was going to come see her. "Dewey will be here," an exasperated Trena finally said, just to placate her. She knew it was a mistake as soon as the words left her mouth, but thought she could get away with the white lie just once. Of course, Diamond looked out from the stage to see if she could spot me. "Where's Dewey?" she asked her mother afterward. "You said he would be here!" Trena tried to convince her that I had been there all along, standing in the back, that she just hadn't seen me before I had to leave, but Diamond knew better. Her trust had been broken, and the betrayal, in her eyes, was mine; *I* had betrayed her. I knew that she had to kill a certain part of herself to deal with me. Diamond had become a part of my world through no choice of her own, and she had to become cold to survive it or have her small heart broken over and over again. I got it. But that didn't make it hurt any less, and no matter how many times I said the words or wrote *I love you* to her in a card or letter, Diamond never allowed herself to say them back to me. All I could do was keep loving her in the hope that she would come back around. Trena warned me that I was in for a tough journey.

"She doesn't trust men," Trena explained. Diamond's daddy hadn't been a constant in her life, her uncle had been locked up since before she was born, and her grandfather passed away just a couple years after Trena and I married. He and Trena had rented a two-bedroom apartment together to split expenses, figuring they could make ends meet with his Social Security check and her child support. When he got cancer, Trena had taken care of him, even though chronic, debilitating stomach problems were starting to take a toll on her. Once her father was gone, though, Trena could no longer afford the place on her own, and she ended up in a cheap one-bedroom unit with Diamond, mother and daughter sharing the same double bed they always had.

I SUPPOSE MOST PEOPLE SAY THIS, but our marriage started out strong and beautiful. We were young and vibrant and were that certain our love could overcome every obstacle that my imprisonment put in our way. Trena would come to Sing Sing three times a week, happy-go-lucky and eager to take care of me, even if it meant just heating up a frozen cheeseburger in the visitors' microwave. We would sit and read my Qu'ran and her Bible together. Faith was the compass in both of our lives, and we saw it as a common denominator despite our different choices. Conversion wasn't on the table. I let Trena be Trena, and she let me be me.

But prison has a way of killing the spirit between two people, no matter how strong faith itself is. The days and months and years go by, and you have to watch the person you care most about in the world grow tired and stressed out and age before your eyes because of you and your position, and there's nothing you can do about it. It was that powerlessness that got to me and ate away at me from the inside. Worst of all was watching from the sidelines as Trena's health deteriorated. Sometimes her stomach hurt so much that she would double over in pain. She was sent from specialist to specialist, test to test, and nothing seemed to help. "I'm missing so much work, I'm going to lose my job, and then what?" she reluctantly told me. It was clear that she could no longer work full-time, but qualifying for disability was a long, red-tape nightmare. As Trena grew more depressed, I started to shut down, too. I was a master of hard-core survival, but I had none of the coping skills you need to keep a relationship alive. I didn't want to hear about the car breaking down and Trena almost getting into an accident, because there was not a damn thing I could do about it. I couldn't do shit about mechanics taking advantage of her, and I couldn't handle the frustration of not being able to stand up for her. I couldn't comfort her when worry kept her awake at night. Even little things tore me up inside, like listening to Trena tell me how hard it was to carry the laundry up and down the stairs. Trena took my lack of response as indifference and a lack of empathy, but trying to explain how inadequate I felt would only have deepened my shame. An emotional wall more foreboding than any prison fence sprang up between us. There were times when I could tell she needed a break from coming up to the prison. "Get out of here," I told her. "Get the fuck away for a while." When you looked at it in the harsh artificial light that Sing Sing cast, Trena and I weren't in this together at all: I didn't have to worry about having enough money to feed my child or pay for whatever medicine I needed; I never had to wonder whether I would have a roof over my head next week or next month. I was the state's problem. But Trena, by the vows I had taken, was mine.

And I was failing her.

When we had first gotten married, Trena and I decided to start trying to have a baby as soon as possible. With our first conjugal visit a whole year away, Trena had elected to have surgery to remove benign fibroids to improve her chances of getting pregnant, given the limited time we were allotted for trailer visits. Both of us are crazy about kids; other inmates' children would always run up to me in the visiting room and wrap themselves around my legs or beg me to pick them up, and Trena was a magnet, too. I could see what a wonderful mother she was, and nothing made me happier than

the idea of becoming a father. I wanted to know what uncondi-
tional love felt like, to give love and be given it in return. I wanted
to coach a Little League team, attend a dance recital, say prayers
at bedtime, unwrap presents on Christmas morning. I wanted to
watch my son or daughter graduate from college, be successful in
life, get married, and bring home a grandchild for Trena and me to
spoil. The promise of having a child made the future seem real. It
was after one of our first trailer visits, in 1997, that Trena visited
Sing Sing, her eyes sparkling.

"I'm late," she announced.

"You mean we could be having a baby?" I asked. The excitement
carried me away and for days, I just lived inside my head, happily
fantasizing about the child—*my child*—coming into the world. Just
the thought of parenthood made every breath I drew in my stale
cell sweet and pure. When Trena got her period, I fell into such
a deep funk that Trena didn't dare tell me when she thought she
might be pregnant again. Years later, she would admit that it was
easier to weather the false alarms alone than to watch my hopes
rise and fall like that again.

Her gynecologist assured Trena that her eggs were fine, and the
fibroids, which had grown back, were not an issue. She never told
her doctor why it was that her husband never came with her to any
of her appointments.

"Dewey, it may be that *you* can't have children," Trena finally
ventured. I didn't want to hear that at all; I suppose no man does.
The suggestion felt like an attack on my masculinity, and I refused
to even discuss the possibility with Trena. It's not like there are any
fertility clinics in the prison system anyway, so the state of my re-
productive system was a moot question. We would just have to keep
trying and keep praying.

Recollecting that long, troubled stretch of our marriage hurts even now, years later, and it feels like an ache that has become a permanent part of me, a hole in my heart that will never heal. I wish I had taken that blow like a fighter, but I didn't. I crumpled in anger and pain, and I came very close to ruining the one good thing that had happened in my life: I pushed Trena away when we needed each other the most. When she underwent exploratory surgery for her stomach problems, the reality of our prison marriage hit her hard—she was married, but she was alone. I couldn't hold her hand before she was wheeled into the operating room, or smile and reassure her I'd be waiting right there when she got out. I couldn't comfort her in the middle of the night when the pain felt like daggers in her gut. I couldn't take care of Diamond when her mother was sick. Dwelling on what I couldn't change, on who I couldn't be because I was locked up, served no purpose, so I did what I'd conditioned myself to do after close to two decades in prison: I pushed the humiliation into a mental lockbox. Trena read my fear as a lack of compassion. "You think it's a form of weakness," she concluded. It wasn't just the baby issue, she argued. She also felt that I had all but brushed off her father's death, and I had offered little comfort as she grieved. "I only know what I know," I told her. "I am what I am."

I WAS STILL TWO YEARS AWAY FROM MY FIRST PAROLE HEARING when I overheard some guys in the yard talking about something called the Innocence Project. They said that volunteer lawyers were getting freedom for the wrongfully convicted, even for some on death row. I headed for the prison law library, hoping to find out more. Since none of the congressmen I'd written to or organizations like the

NAACP had answered my pleas for help, the Innocence Project might be a new avenue for me to explore. In the library, I asked the law clerk if he'd ever heard of them.

"They do DNA testing," he told me.

"What do you mean, DNA?" I asked.

The science of extracting and matching DNA hadn't even existed in 1977 when Emma Crapser was killed, but I knew from the police files that during my first trial, my attorneys had obtained evidence recovered from the crime scene, including the chisel and cloth and other items used to strangle the victim, which could potentially hold biological proof that I wasn't the killer. William O'Neill told the jury during my trial that DNA evidence had been recovered, without saying it hadn't been tested, or that there was no DNA proof in hand linking me to the murder. It was courtroom theatrics: the prosecutor didn't need any scientific proof when he knew that sly innuendo alone would convince the jury. He just let the jury falsely assume that the samples must have been linked to the accused, because why else would O'Neill have brought them up?

The Innocence Project was founded by Barry C. Scheck and Peter Neufeld at the Benjamin Cardozo School of Law at Yeshiva University in New York City in 1992. Scheck became famous a couple of years later as a key defense witness in the O.J. Simpson trial, where he cast doubts on the police and laboratory mishandling of DNA evidence that allegedly tied the football Hall of Famer to the murders of his estranged wife, Nicole, and Ron Brown, a waiter friend who had dropped by her town house that night to return a pair of sunglasses Nicole had left at a neighborhood restaurant. Like the rest of America, everybody inside Sing Sing followed the Simpson trial on television like a daily soap opera. People were all comparing their case to O.J.'s. We were all rooting for the Juice to get cut loose. We assumed that the L.A. police were railroading him because they had proved themselves to be racist thugs in the beating of Rodney King. The white minority and Aryans inside Sing Sing knew to lie low during the Simpson trial, and when he got acquitted, everyone applauded and whooped for joy. I felt as if I had gotten a chance to see and understand real law: if I had the money O.J. did, I'd have gotten out. My innocence didn't count anywhere near as much as my ability to fight for it.

In the decade since the Simpson case, DNA testing had gotten progressively more advanced and precise. Since I had exhausted all my appeals, the Innocence Project looked like it might be my last resort. I knew I had never been in Emma Crapser's building and had never met her. There was no way in hell I could be linked by any DNA evidence to the crime scene or the victim. Maybe a forensic heavy hitter like Barry Scheck could help provide the biological proof that would exonerate me. All it would take was just one righteous crusader to fight for me and fight for the truth. I dug up an address for the Innocence Project and began writing them letters, imploring them to take on my case. I filled page after page with my story, writing it out in my neatest longhand, only to do it all over again the following week when I hadn't heard anything back. I vowed to keep writing until I had an answer.

I HAD MY FIRST PAROLE HEARING IN JANUARY 2003. I waited for the board to review my file and take note of twenty years of good behavior, of all the certificates I had earned in an effort to improve myself, of my too-brief but glorious prison boxing career. There were three parole commissioners. They asked if I was sorry I had killed Emma Crapser. I felt my chest tighten. I knew they wanted to hear me express remorse. I knew that one lie might be my ticket to freedom, same as it had been when the district attorney had dangled his deal in front of me while the jury was deliberating during my second trial. I hadn't changed my mind or my heart since then. Truth is truth.

"I can't say I'm sorry for something I didn't do," I replied. "I'm innocent."

You could tell whether you got parole by the thickness of the envelope that came in the mail a few days after the hearing. Guys would feel it before opening it. Thick meant the papers for appeal were inside and you got hit; thin meant you were going home. Mine was thick. I opened it and read the verdict. My fate was sealed in five sentences:

Parole is denied, hold 24 months. Next appearance 01/05 Board.

Reasons: After careful consideration of your file and personal interview, parole is denied. The instant offense represents a serious escalation of your prior criminal activity, during the course of the instant offense, you caused the death of another human being, note is made of your positive institutional record, however, your release at this time would deprecate the serious nature of your crime and undermine public confidence in the Criminal Justice System. Commissioners concur.

I was pissed off. I threw the letter down, then filled out the appeal papers, praying something would pop up in my favor. Nothing did, and the appeal, too, was denied.

Trena and I had been careful not to build up our expectations or to invest too much emotional coin in the daydreams we had,

nearly ten years into our marriage, of finally setting up a real life together as husband and wife. But I could tell she was crestfallen. "If
they want me to tell them I did it," I warned her, "then I'm going
to die in prison." She nodded sadly in agreement but held fiercely to
her own faith in a power greater than the justice system.

"Don't give up," she urged. "Keep fighting! We're going to get
you out of here."

She still hadn't looked at the file I had tried to show her when
we first met, but I had tucked occasional clippings or bits of docu-
mentation into my letters to her every now and then, hoping to
pique her curiosity.

When I was eighteen years old with a friend Allison.
My only picture from my youth before going to prison. 1977.

Shariff is the man who helped change my life in prison. 1985.

Me and Trena on our wedding day, March 30, 1996.

Trena, Diamond, and me when we became a family. 1996.

Graduating college with a bachelor's degree in 2005.

Class of 2006, New York Theological Seminary in Professional Studies. (above)

On my way to the International Boxing Hall of Fame. 2013. (left)

Trena, Diamond, and me during a cookout after my release. 2014.

I tattooed my back so I would never forget
how much work went into my freedom. 2014.

Getting ready for trial. This is the team at
WilmerHale who helped me win my case. 2015.

I spoke before a group of law enforcement officials in Brazil about passing a law for the wrongfully convicted. 2015.

Ready to hang glide in Brazil. 2015.

10

PEOPLE WHO DON'T KNOW MUCH ABOUT BOXING usually think that brute force is what wins a fight, but that's only the half of it. How much you can take and whether you stay standing are just as critical as how hard you can hit. Every blow teaches you something about your opponent. It doesn't matter whether you lose or how beat-up and bloody and weary to the damn bone you are: as long as you pull yourself off those ropes, you finish a stronger man than you were when you stepped into the ring. No one ever knocked me out. No one.

Not long after my parole was denied, the state changed my status, deciding that I wasn't enough of a threat to warrant maximum security and should be transferred from Sing Sing to a medium-security prison. I ended up in Fishkill, which was only a few minutes' drive from Trena's apartment. If either of us thought the change in environment and closer proximity to each other would improve things on the personal front, though, we couldn't have been more wrong. We argued and sometimes went for days—seventeen, once—without speaking, each of us convinced there was no way the other could possibly understand where we were coming from or what we were going through. There was a lot of truth in that, too. I always thought marriage meant your troubles were shared, your load lightened, but prison has its own algebra, and struggles get multiplied—not divided—by two. Trena and I retreated to our separate corners, trying to catch our breath.

Our turn came around for a trailer visit at Fishkill, and Trena stayed away. A knockout punch. Throwing that kind of shade was the worst kind of rejection, and from my humiliated perspective, it seemed like the ultimate power play. By leaving me alone in my cell, she all but told me that I may be her husband, but at the end of the day, I was still just inmate 84A0172. A lot of our difficulty revolved around not being able to conceive. Trena complained that I was selfish and cold. I had pinned all the blame on her for not having a baby, not appreciating all the doctors' visits, lab tests, and surgeries she had gone through alone in the effort to conceive. No matter how hard I tried, I couldn't seem to get across how much fatherhood mattered to me, that it wasn't just some blown-up macho pride doing a number on me. Maybe you have to have lived most of your life unwanted to even feel a want this deep. I figured she didn't care as much as I did and even thought that she couldn't, because she already had a child. My life had been marked by sorrow and disappointment at nearly every turn, and I learned in prison how to create my own positive, to start from emotional scratch and raise myself to become the man I wanted to be. But this obstacle seemed insurmountable. How had my excitement and yearning to be a father, to offer up my heart as wholly as any human being can, turned into something so bitter and lonely? I couldn't wrap my head around what was happening to Trena and me. Rocky as our marriage had become, I knew our only chance of making it was if we could be together. Getting out of prison, becoming a free man, wasn't just some dream, some fantasy movie to flick on in my imagination to make the miserable hours pass more easily. It was my vocation. My job. I couldn't afford to slack off and wallow in self-pity. Each week, I wrote another letter to the Innocence Project.

Four years after sending off my first letter, I finally got a polite but terse response in the mail: *Don't write us anymore. We've got you on our list.*

I had no way of knowing then how long that list was: more than three thousand inmates a year write to ask for help from the Innocence Project, it turns out, and at any given time, they're evaluating between six thousand and eight thousand potential cases. I had no idea where I was in line or what they were going to do next, but at least it seemed like I had escaped the flat-out rejection pile and made it into their "maybe" stack. There's only so much you can do from inside prison to clear your name, and I'd lost contact with my old lawyer Mickey Steiman after the higher courts had turned down all his attempts to appeal my conviction. I didn't have any civil rights organizations or celebrities crusading for my release, no fund-raising benefit concerts or even outraged friends and family demanding justice for Dewey Bozella. The vague note from the Innocence Project didn't amount to a promise or anything close to encouragement, but it was the only flicker of interest I'd had in my case in years. I was pleased but tried at the same time not to let myself get too worked up about it. I'd known ever since I was little how hope can turn to hurt in the blink of an eye.

I never pushed Trena to become my advocate—I wanted her to come to that on her own, if she was going to—but as time wore on, it got harder and harder for me to accept her choice to stay out of my legal battles, to be my wife instead of my warrior.

"Do you really want me to come home?" I heatedly demanded one day. Plenty of friends of mine were in prison relationships where the women actually preferred to have their men stay behind bars. That way, they didn't have to worry about them getting into trouble on the streets, or coming home drunk or high, or messing around with other women. If they were disrespectful or wanted to pick a fight, all the wife or girlfriend had to do was turn around, drive back out the prison gate, and go home. She decides whether to visit, and when they see each other, everything is about how hot she looks, and how much he wants her, and how grateful he is that she brought him the Snickers and cigarettes he asked for. You wonder what the story is on all those lonely-hearts prison groupies who seek out inmate romances? Control and containment, plain and simple. I knew damn well Trena wasn't like that, but when we were foundering, my doubts threatened to get the best of me, and it was an easy button to push.

"How can you even ask that?" Trena retorted, offended by my cheap shot. She had a daughter to take care of and didn't have money to hire lawyers or private investigators, anyway. Her health was a constant worry, as well; she had had four operations while I was locked up, and her chronic stomach pain had put her on permanent disability. There was a period where things got so bleak that Diamond, then a teenager, was supporting the both of them on her minimum-wage paycheck from McDonald's, turning it over to her mama each week without a word of complaint. Diamond had a purity of heart that filled me with both love and fatherly fear. With her high cheekbones, doe eyes, and tall, willowy build, strangers were always wondering if she was a model. Diamond is demure—Trena had raised her only child to have strong morals—but I worried about the wolves lurking in the shadows out there, and I wished I could protect her as she blossomed into a beautiful young woman. We had our father-daughter talks in a visiting room full of convicted rapists, killers, con artists, and thieves. When Diamond started dating and telling me about the boys she liked, I offered advice gleaned from the hostile street world I had known at her age.

"First and foremost, you have to ask yourself: Is he good?" I told her. "Is he putting his hands on you? Is he treating you with respect? If he's not respecting you, you don't need to be around him. Is he taking away your dreams? Then step away. Don't let him tell you what to do. If you're ever in a situation that scares you, don't you be afraid to come to your mother or me and we'll handle it for you."

Diamond could only nod in agreement. She never shot back and said what we both knew she might have, if she had had that kind of mean streak: *Why would I come to you for help? What could you do?* From her lifetime of knowing me, I was, as a father figure, all talk. The ghost at the school play.

If you want real irony, though, there's this: from Trena's point of view, the very same traits that made me a model prisoner also made me a difficult soul mate. After the Muslims steered me away from my street-thug mentality, I worked hard to learn to keep my emotions in check, to avoid confrontation, and to choke down hurt and anger. Boxing had given me discipline, and I had found an emotional outlet in writing, performing, and directing plays through a prison program called Rehabilitation Through the Arts. Both those passions helped me to mentally scale the prison walls, to let my body and my imagination take over and fly me to a different place and a different life. But marriage doesn't come with a referee or a script, and I couldn't get the words or the footwork right anymore. After Trena had shined on one of our conjugal visits and after weeks of constant bickering, I impulsively petitioned for a transfer to another facility, wanting to flee the discord. I felt spiteful enough not to mention it to my wife.

RIGHT AROUND OUR NINTH ANNIVERSARY, Trena had to undergo a partial hysterectomy, which put an end to our dreams for a baby. That same year, 2005, I came before the parole board for a second time. It was like an instant replay of the first hearing: the board demanded again that I admit guilt and express remorse for the murder of Emma Crapser. Once again, I proclaimed my innocence and got another two years tacked on to my sentence. I returned to my cell with the grim realization that I could easily end up repeating this Groundhog Day drill every two years until I eventually died behind bars. They were sentencing me to death two years at a time. I remember it was a Friday afternoon. Come Monday, an envelope from the Innocence Project arrived in the mail.

"We have accepted your case," the letter informed me. They were launching their investigation and would be in touch.

Shit, it's about time, I thought. There was no jubilation, no heart soar of hope. The stalemates with both Trena and the parole board had sapped whatever optimism I had left. I had worked myself into a mad funk. I was mad about everything. Too mad to even be grateful for the people who were on my side. I hated the way I could feel the anger seeping in, like a dampness in the walls. This wasn't who I was or how I wanted to be, but neither prayer nor my small library of motivational books were helping this time. By that point, the prison-boxing program had been defunct for five years, so that outlet was gone. I'd completed so many programs and classes that I had a master's degree already, and budget cuts meant there was next to nothing left to sign up for, nothing to distract my mind and keep it occupied on something other than the unfair hands life kept dealing me. The Innocence Project can never predict how long it will take to investigate and litigate a new case. Some are closed in a year, and others drag on for a decade. All I could do was wait, and pray, and fume.

Even if I was scarred enough to hold my optimism in check, Trena surprised me with her excitement over the Innocence Project news when I showed her the letter. It seemed to provide an affirmation for her, and for the first time, she allowed herself to engage in the battle for my freedom. She asked questions, read the documents I had, and studied the old newspaper clips I had saved. It felt good to finally have her, heart and soul, on my side.

Technically, Fishkill may have been considered easier time than Sing Sing, but to me, it was a whole lot worse. Many of the guys at Fishkill were finishing out their sentences, and I was constantly surrounded by conversations about who was going home and what they were going to do when they got out. They talked about all the steaks that they were going to eat, all the soft beds they were going to sleep in, all the nice cars they were going to drive, all the family and friends who were going to be waiting for them. Even with the Innocence Project working my case, my tunnel felt dark and endless, and I couldn't see that kind of light yet. The Fishkill population was also younger, more arrogant. Inmates were content to lounge in the dayroom and watch old Bullwinkle the Moose cartoons for hours. I couldn't relate to them the way I could the old lifers at Sing Sing, the ones determined to better themselves, to find some sense of purpose and meaning even when freedom wasn't on the table. And it wasn't just the inmates at Fishkill who were cocky; the guards were just as bad. Even Trena bristled under their constant badgering during visitation: *You're sitting too close, you can't kiss him like that, you need to go out and change because your bra clasp is setting off the metal detector.*

One morning, my long-forgotten transfer request suddenly came through without warning. Before I had a chance to tell Trena what was happening, I was an hour away and being processed into the small medium-security state prison in Otisville. She was furious at first, but did a complete turnaround once she laid eyes on the place. Otisville was an unimposing low-slung beige prison out in the sticks of Orange County, not far from the Catskills. The whole atmosphere at Otisville had a lazy vibe to it. Even the guards were laid-back. Trena showed up one time in sweatpants that clung like leggings, and the guards just waved her through with a friendly, "All right, Ms. B, just don't wear those again!" There were no trailers, but the visiting room was smaller and calmer, and the overall peacefulness sat well with Trena.

Not with me.

The slow burn I'd been working up at Fishkill hit a fast boil in Otisville. It was like a damn criminal retirement home. Just like at Fishkill, nobody was doing anything there, and for whatever pent-up reason, I took the collective lack of ambition personally. The inmates all just watched TV, played cards, and napped the day away either stretched out on the gym floor or with their heads down on the tables in the mess hall. There was gym equipment, but it sat gathering dust. There was a track, but every year some dude would collapse and die just walking around it. One goddamn old man dropped dead of a heart attack one time when I was out there jogging. They brought the ambulance and trucks out and spent twenty minutes trying to make like he was alive and they were trying to resuscitate him, but we all knew he was dead the minute the poor bastard hit the ground. Truth be told, the whole place had a dead, spiritless atmosphere. I would wake up in the morning and go down the hill to work out, and my whole body changed as I went through my sets; there was no energy, no one to partner with so we could urge each other on, and I would get bored and quit. Pushing my body to its limits had always pumped up my mood before, but now even working up a good sweat was dragging me down, pulling me under so I could barely breathe. *What the fuck am I going down there for?* I would ask myself. *I'm the only guy working out, hitting the bag, jumping rope. I can't deal with this shit. There's nothing here. This is horrible, man. I gotta get out of here.* If I ended up in prison for life, it couldn't be here, where the opiate dullness would slowly sap the strength from me, both mind and body. Crazy as it sounds, I began lobbying to get sent back to Sing Sing. I was used to being around activity and noise, I needed that *engagement*, the hivelike buzz of life. The prison bureaucracy quickly shut me down: you don't go from medium security to maximum security unless you become a danger to others; we weren't transferring junior colleges here. I would have to suck it up. There was no choice left. I got my certification to help the cooks as a sort of sous chef and started working in the mess hall. The job did little to take the edge off my restlessness.

One day, I walked into the cafeteria in a storm-cloud mood and slammed the door purposefully, startling awake the men dozing with their heads on the tables.

Yo, yo man, what you do that for?

"Damn, man, you're all killing me!" I bellowed. "Playin' cards. Watching TV. I'm active, and I can't be around people not doing shit!"

My frustration was just the scab over the deeper wound of fatherhood lost. Lying on my hard bunk in prison's relentless twilight, I let the familiar old self-pity swamp me. *Damn, man, how am I supposed to deal with this shit? Everybody has a fucking legacy. I don't have shit. Who the fuck does Dewey have as a legacy? Dewey has nobody.*

Faith didn't even come into the picture. God didn't have anything to do with this, as far as I was concerned. This was my issue. I put myself into my own prison, the walled-off world within, a personal lockdown that shut out everyone and everything else. Yeah, I might have been selfish, and I sure as hell didn't mean to take it out on Trena, but I was reeling from the pain and I did. At the end of the day, I wasn't sure that fatherhood was something I ever could get over, a dream I could give up. *I love you, I love you, I love you. But I need time to think,* I silently implored Trena. I didn't want to turn my back on this woman, but I needed time to be by myself, to turn this problem over in my mind. *What's wrong with that?* I argued with the invisible debate partner who'd lived in my head for twenty years and counting. I had pinned all my hopes on becoming a father to get through my bid. When I imagined myself exonerated someday, walking through the prison gates into the life that had been stolen from me, what I saw was a family waiting for me. And if justice was never served, and if I did end up spending the rest of my life in prison, fatherhood would at least give me one chance to leave something positive behind, to love unconditionally and be loved back that same way. It was my light. I couldn't just turn it off and pretend it didn't matter. Boxing had taught me to focus, to never back down. It had made me a man. But it was time to find a validation outside the ring, my identity beyond these bars. I wasn't the same young punk who had entered Sing Sing. I was middle-aged now. I was maturing, but it wasn't a natural process. I had no

blueprint to go by, no lifetime of real-world experiences and relationships. Emotions were a minefield I had to map on my own, and
I had to grope my way across in the dark on my hands and knees.

After a while, I felt calm enough to take out my pen and sit
down to write Trena a long letter. I told her I needed time to think
this shit out, that this was something serious to me. That this was
my issue. *Can I live the rest of my life without children?* I wrote. *Nothing can make up for your own child,* I concluded. Nothing.

Trena was both wounded and furious when she read my words.
Infertility had been testing our marriage for years by then, and with
pregnancy now out of the question for her, she figured this was my
way of kicking her to the curb for a younger girlfriend, that I was
telling her to move on with her life and find someone nice who
deserved her, because I needed to find someone who could bear
my children. That I was ready to throw away the wife I had for the
child I didn't.

She didn't write back or show up on visiting day to confront
me. When I tried to call—collect was the only way—she refused the
charges. I kept trying, and she changed her phone number. My letters came back unopened. My life and future were as unresolved
as ever, but Trena acted with a certainty that left no doubt in my
mind: she'd had enough.

THEN MY BID FOR FREEDOM SLAMMED INTO A BRICK WALL, TOO: Olga Akselrod,
the attorney assigned to oversee my case at the Innocence Project,
arrived for a visit one day in December of 2007. It had been two
whole years since the Innocence Project had agreed to take me on,
and I wondered what news she might be bringing. Maybe they'd
found the scientific evidence to prove I'd been falsely accused and

sent away for a murder I had nothing to do with and were ready to file a motion for a new trial. I was surprised when I walked into the visiting room and saw three young associates sitting with Olga. They all looked nervous as hell. We exchanged pleasantries, and I sat down. Olga cut right to the chase.

"There is no DNA, Dewey. The state destroyed all the physical evidence in your case. I'm sorry."

The Innocence Project only took on DNA investigations. They were going to have to drop me. Olga rushed on even as I tried to absorb the devastating news.

"It's not over yet," she said. They had spent nearly two years combing through police reports, interrogations, depositions, trial transcripts, and news reports surrounding the Crapser murder, and they were convinced of my innocence. So certain of it, in fact, Olga continued, that they did something almost unheard of within the Innocence Project: they went looking for a private law firm with the manpower, political clout, and deep pockets it would take to pursue my case pro bono. Wilmer Cutler Pickering Hale and Dorr had agreed to step up. A prestigious Park Avenue firm with a thousand lawyers on three continents, WilmerHale was as far out of my league as you could possibly get and still be in this solar system. These were Ivy League cats who advised presidents. They argued before the Supreme Court—and won. They had an international client list full of people who traveled by private jet and watched the World Series from VIP box seats. One of their partners was considered the father of Legal Aid. The firm's pedigree might have intimidated me if I had known it at the time, but all I knew right then was that the three attorneys Olga had brought with her—two men and a woman, all in their twenties—were asking if I would let them look into my case. For free.

Hell to the yes.

"Art Regula," I said first thing to my new lawyers. "He was the guy out to get me." For the next three hours, I poured out my whole story, my words tripping over one another as I tried to summarize the thirty years since that Poughkeepsie detective had collared me on the street. Ross Firsenbaum, the WilmerHale junior associate who had convinced his bosses to let him take on my case when the Innocence Project approached the firm, was just twenty-seven years old, quiet and shy seeming, with fierce black brows that framed kind brown eyes. Ross scribbled down notes and tried to get a question in edgewise now and then, but I couldn't stop rambling. It felt like I was in a dream and had to get my whole long story out fast before I woke up and this chance disappeared. After we got to know each other, Ross told me that all three of them had been stunned when they left Otisville, and the woman associate had cried most of the way back to Manhattan. "This is just step one," Ross cautioned me before they left that afternoon, "and we don't even know what two, three, and four are going to be yet.

"This is going to be a long process," he said. "We'll be in touch."

"Art Regula," I reminded him.

I longed to share the good news with Trena, but we were still estranged, and the possibility of divorce was slowly pressing down on us. The only reason we hadn't actually discussed it was that we still weren't speaking.

TRENA STAYED AWAY FOR SIX MONTHS. My old friend Allen Thomas, who had been such a mentor to my late brother Leon, came by to visit and offer his wisdom. Allen knew I would listen to him even if I acted like I wasn't, that I would at least take what he had to say out to ponder later, in the quiet of my cell. Now he sat across from me and shook his gray head.

"Boy, you're making a big mistake," he said with a sigh. Marriage to a good woman like Trena wasn't something to discard when things weren't perfect. I had better find a way to set things right, he warned, or I would regret it for the rest of my life. I stewed in my own juices for a while, but I knew Allen was right. Not long after he left, I reached out to a friend's wife, someone Trena would answer the door to, and asked her to go urge Trena to come talk to me. She obliged, but I didn't get the response I'd hoped for.

"Nah, tell him to have a great life," was the answer Trena relayed back.

I wrote a letter saying I knew I had made a mistake, I was sorry, and I wanted to apologize face-to-face. I asked her to bring Diamond so I could apologize to her, too, for the turmoil I had caused in our family. This time the letter didn't come back unopened, and when the guards told me one day that I had a visitor, I felt a rush of joy. Maybe we could rebuild what we once had. Trena showed up alone, in a little black dress that neatly hugged every stunning curve of her. She had lost more than fifty pounds, and her svelte figure made my jaw drop.

"Oh my," I spluttered like a dumbstruck teenager picking up his date for the prom. "You look really beautiful." She gave me a look that told me she knew it and didn't need my endorsement.

Humbled, I asked her to come back, for her and Diamond to be my family again. Trena played it cool and distant.

"I gotta think about it," she said before unfolding herself like Audrey Hepburn from the sorry plastic chair. I gaped after her as she sailed through the door back into the real world. A month passed before she showed up again. She forgave me, but she also laid down the law.

"That was your last time," she warned. "I don't know what it was you had to find out, but you better be sure you know what you know."

I knew I couldn't live without this woman in my life, that she was worth the sacrifice I would have to make. I would be a husband, not a father.

IN 2007, I CAME UP FOR PAROLE FOR A THIRD TIME.

Do you have any remorse for the murder of Emma Crapser?

I'm sorry she was murdered, she didn't deserve to die that way, but I didn't do it.

Parole denied.

Two more years tacked on. I looked at the listless young men dozing away their days at Otisville and knew I was about to snap. I could feel a fury building inside me, pushing its way to the surface, and it scared me. I felt overwhelmed by a despair that finally had me on the ropes. My gut told me to isolate myself and I asked to be sent to solitary so I could have time to work my way through this fresh, raw pain. It was the primal need of a wounded animal, to find a safe hiding place where the vultures couldn't smell defeat. This request, too, was denied. The box was supposed to be a form of punishment, not some personal Zen retreat for introspective inmates.

One morning, a sergeant drove up in his van while I was on my way to rec, fixated on finding a way to get out of Otisville. When he stopped to ask me something, I asked him what I had to do to get sent to the box.

"All you gotta do is refuse to work, disobey a direct order," he shrugged.

"That's what I'm doing, then." I climbed into his van.

"Let's go, let's go," I said.

"What're you doing, Bozella? Get the hell out," he ordered me. I disobeyed.

"Are you serious?" the sergeant demanded.

"I'm serious, man. I gotta be around people who are serious, man. These kids are killing me."

He drove me to the administrative building, where I was charged for disobeying a direct order. From there, I was taken to Fishkill for a hearing. The supervisor at Fishkill was surprised to see one of his model prisoners and wondered what I was doing.

"Listen, I don't want to go back to Otisville," I confided. My infraction carried a penalty of thirty days of solitary in the Special Housing Unit, but I knew that wasn't severe enough to change my status back to the higher-risk status I needed to get back to Fishkill for good. "Can I get back in population here?" I implored the supervisor. "Give me the time I need to be disqualified from going back. Give me forty-five days." To my relief, he agreed. Fishkill wasn't Sing Sing, but at least it had some opportunities that Otisville didn't for school, volunteer work, and Christian ministry programs once I came out of solitary.

But it turned out that the peace I craved was the last thing I found in my self-imposed exile. A twenty-one-year-old Blood had just been brought in and was putting up a nonstop racket, screaming and hollering to his homeboys locked up on the same block. The COs finally had enough of it and decided that it might calm him down to put him in a cell with me. So much for solitary. I was mad as shit. Who made me Daddy Day-Care? As soon as the kid stepped into my cell—our cell, now—he was mouthing off, in my face, and angling for a fight.

"Yo, man, I gotta sleep on the top bunk?" he complained, climbing up. "I don't want to sleep on no top bunk." He started up with his hollering again, calling out to his homeboys in other cells till they got their own little gangster shit chorale going.

Oh my God, don't tell me I'm gonna have to kick this kid's ass, I thought miserably.

"Yo, you get down. I gotta talk to you," I said calmly, but with enough command to let the punk know it would be a bad idea to cross me.

The kid slid down and glared at me.

"Listen, all this hollering and screaming is not going to solve the problem," I explained reasonably. "I been doing this for nearly twenty-five years. I got twenty years to life, man. At night, you need to be respectful. At night, no hollering and screaming at your people. The reason I'm in the bottom bunk, man, is because I was here first. You know how it is. So let's stop with the bullshit, man. I'm trying to go home."

Home. Young and belligerent as he was, I saw that he grasped the meaning of that word to me, the chance he was taking away if he picked a fight and got the both of us written up. He fell quiet then.

"Man, I understand," he finally replied, though I doubt he really got it. "I understand, I understand. Twenty-five years?"

We spent the next two weeks together in that cell, talking. I never asked why he was in prison and he never told me. He did tell me that he had cut a guy across the face to get in a gang and had gotten three years added on to his sentence. That was the price he was willing to pay for the life insurance policy of sorts that gang membership bought him. I talked about boxing and he'd listen like a kid at library story hour, wanting to hear about my bouts, about my brief stint at Floyd Patterson's camp when I was young. When we weren't talking, he saw me reading all the time. "Yo, man, you think you could help me with this?" he asked, showing me the GED workbook he'd been given. I walked him through the exercises. "Don't give up, man," I urged the kid when he got frustrated. "I was a school dropout in the tenth grade, no better than you. I did all the wrong things. If I can change, you can do it. It's going to be hard, but you can't give up. Just work on your weak points every day for one hour. One hour. If you don't understand a word, ask me and I'll help you to the best of my abilities." I spoke to him as an equal, knowing too well how easy it was to make a street kid feel stupid and worthless just by the tone of your voice. There was no more hollering and carrying on. One night I heard his voice drift in a near whisper from the top bunk: "Man, I'm thinking about throwing down my flag."

I'd never know whether he left the Bloods or what became of him after he left the box, but the COs stopped by to thank me for calming him down.

"This kid is looking for attention, for a father figure," I told them. "I know why you put him in the cell with me. I don't like it, but I understand."

TRENA GOT PERMISSION TO VISIT WHILE I WAS IN THE BOX. She had never seen me in shackles and handcuffs. She immediately burst into tears.

"*What* is going on?" she cried.

"Trena, please don't cry," I tried to soothe her. I was frustrated that we were allowed no contact, that I couldn't hug her even briefly. "I'm okay. Just know I'm okay."

"They got you like an animal, Dewey," she sobbed.

"But I'm okay," I kept insisting. "This is not going to stop anything." I knew my sudden reappearance in Fishkill, in lockdown, was scary and confusing to her, especially because she didn't know how and why I got there.

"Listen, baby, there ain't no sense in crying, this is how it is," I told her. "I'd rather be here than where I was, and you're only five minutes away now."

She looked at me through swollen eyes.

"Why'd you leave in the first place, Dewey? Why'd you leave?"

I shook my head, full of regret. "Trena, I was dealing with my own demons," was all I could say. "I didn't make the best decisions."

Things were going to be different now, I promised her.

WilmerHale had found Art Regula.

11

I COULD TELL THAT THE WILMERHALE LAWYERS LISTENING TO MY STORY were young, but I had no idea that first day back in Otisville that they were as green as they were. In fact, they had zero trial experience. They specialized in commercial and securities law. But while he was in college at Amherst, Ross Firsenbaum, the team leader, had attended a presentation by Innocence Project cofounder Peter Neufeld and one of the prisoners the Project had gotten exonerated, and the experience had ignited a passion in him. When the Innocence Project had referred my case to WilmerHale, Ross had pounced on the chance to crusade against injustice, and he lobbied the law firm's partners to let him represent me pro bono. Ross had looked at the forty-five hundred pages of transcripts from both my trials and had reached the same conclusion about the case as the Innocence Project, but the full impact of what he was undertaking, he would later admit, didn't hit him until the long drive back to the city from Otisville that snowy winter day, when one thought lodged frozen in his mind: *How in the world did anyone in the United States of America get convicted with this?* And how, he had to wonder, would a twenty-seven-year-old lawyer with no criminal expe-

rience ever undo such a grave injustice? Whatever confidence my
new legal team lacked at the outset, though, Trena and I more than
made up for with our own dogged optimism. I could tell Ross truly
cared by the intent way he listened to me, asking all the right questions, while we were scrunched up in the humiliating kiddie-sized
wooden chairs kept in the tiny room Otisville used for attorney-
client meetings. That Ross was a smart man was obvious enough,
but just as important to me, looking at him straight in the eye as
I told my story, I believed that he was a good man. The cruelty of
what had happened to me seemed to hit him on a personal level,
and I knew right then I would never be a case number to him.

Back in Manhattan, Ross had formed a team of four attorneys
and a project assistant. He and his team started digging. First off,
they would need to get hold of all the old case files, pore over every
single page, and interview every witness they could still find thirty
years after the murder, all in the hope of ferreting out new evidence
that might exonerate me or be grounds, at least, for a third trial. I
was a legal jigsaw puzzle with countless scattered pieces. Wilmer-
Hale began seeking access to police and D.A. records pertaining to
the Crapser case and the very similar murder of Mary King, only to
be ignored for months at a time. What did they have to hide? The
fierce resistance only made Ross and his team more curious, and
all that much more determined. There were also questions about
what records even still existed, and what had been destroyed since
the cases were considered solved and so much time had passed—the
Internet and its potential for infinite storage in cyberspace didn't
exist when I was convicted, and no bureaucracy has the physical
space to hang on to the mountains of material from every old case
indefinitely.

The team hunkered down to compile a list of witnesses, then

hired a private investigator to try and track them down. Wilmer-Hale discovered that some of the witnesses had died, others were in prison, and still others were in the wind and couldn't be found, but a few were still around. The Poughkeepsie police detective I considered my archenemy, Art Regula, had long since retired. Ross was pleased but surprised when Regula agreed to a meeting and invited the WilmerHale team to come visit him at his home in Dutchess County. My lawyers sat around the former cop's dining room table and explained what they were doing. Ross asked Regula if he could walk him through the Crapser murder and my arrest to the best of his memory.

"I hope you don't mind," Regula rasped in the sandpaper voice that had grilled me for hours at a time when I was just eighteen, "but I refreshed my recollection before you got here."

Ross was taken aback but tried not to show it. Had Regula called his old buddies on the force or compared notes with the D.A.'s office? I had warned Ross that Regula had always had a vendetta against me.

"Refreshed with what?" Ross wondered.

"I kept my case files," Regula answered.

This revelation hit Ross as strange, if not a little suspicious. Why in the hell would a retired cop hang on to old files? Especially cases considered closed nearly twenty years ago? Ross was keen to see what Regula had, but he didn't want to put him on the defensive by coming on too strong.

"Did you keep other case files after you retired?" he asked casually.

"No," Regula replied. "It's the only one."

"Why did you keep this one?" Ross pressed. Regula didn't miss a beat.

"Because I knew someone like you would be at the door some-day, because he didn't do it."

Regula told the lawyers he believed I was innocent once he had learned that the fingerprint found on Ms. Crapser's bathroom window was found to be that of Donald Wise, who by then was serving time for the murder of Mary King and the beating of her two sisters. The Kings lived just three blocks away from Emma Crapser. Although Regula had testified for the prosecution in both my trials, he explained that as a police officer, his testimony was supposed to be limited to the facts, not his opinion about my innocence or guilt, so his doubts had never been revealed. If Regula felt at all responsible for my fate, however, he didn't let on. He was matter-of-fact, not at all emotional, about sharing his conclusions with Ross. The jury, he reasoned, had had the same information about the fingerprint as he did and was aware of Wise's conviction in Mary King's murder.

Regula did, however, recall something that hadn't come out in trial: he told Ross how his partner, Pete Murphy, had interviewed a next-door neighbor who had heard trash cans banging around in the back alley under Emma Crapser's bathroom window the night of her murder. That crucial bit of information had never been written down, Regula said, and was not included in the district attorney's report. My defense had always contended that the mysterious "plumber" who talked his way into Emma Crapser's apartment earlier in the day to check a leak she knew nothing about was, in fact, Donald Wise casing the place and making sure the bathroom window was unlocked so he could slip in later via the side alley, using the trash cans below to boost himself to the second-floor bathroom window. The banging the neighbor reported hearing fit that scenario. Our theory was reinforced by yet another key revelation the WilmerHale team discovered in pages of a police report in the file Regula had given them: Emma Crapser's upstairs neighbors had had company that summer night, with people coming and going through the front door on North Hamilton at the very time that the burglary was taking place if you believed Moseley and Smith. Four separate people reported being up and having eyes on the street during the time frame of the murder, and not a single one of them saw anyone out in front of 15 North Hamilton, though the testimony that convicted me from Lamar Smith and Wayne Moseley would have had five black teenagers supposedly loitering there—the Smith brothers watching from across the street, Pittman walking up and down the sidewalk as lookout, and Moseley and me allegedly breaking in through the front door (Moseley said he kicked it until it "just busted open") and then breaking into Ms. Crapser's apartment door just inside. No one but the Smith brothers reported seeing two guys run out of the building around the time of the murder, or hearing me supposedly holler at the lookout, Sweet Pea Pittman, for failing to warn us that the old lady had been dropped off and was heading inside.

A seventeen-year-old neighbor girl interviewed in Regula's police report even said she personally knew the Smiths and Pittman and had not seen any of the three that night while she was sitting outside on a bench on Ms. Crapser's block. She remembered being there until eleven o'clock.

Statements in the Regula report also directly contradicted the dubious get-out-of-jail-free testimony by Lamar Smith and Moseley that two doors were broken to get inside the Crapser apartment. By their own account, Moseley and Smith were hardly in any shape to have been keen observers: Moseley estimated on the stand that he had been "pretty high" on marijuana and "pretty drunk" after downing "anywhere in between from eight to fourteen quarts of beer" in Mansion Park with Smith, Pittman, and me before supposedly going to rob Emma Crapser that night. During trial, both Ms. Crapser's niece and the officer who first responded to the niece's emergency call said there was no apparent damage to either the outside door or the apartment door. In Regula's report, the neighbors, who had been letting their guests in and out all evening, said the same.

Ross got in touch with my original attorney, Mickey Steiman, to ask about the new material he had found in the Regula report. Mickey, it turned out, had been so disheartened by the miscarriage of justice in my case that he gave up criminal law altogether after I was convicted for the second time. Had Mickey been aware of the statements neighbors had given police contradicting the accounts of Lamar Smith and Wayne Moseley? Ross wondered.

Mickey was dumbfounded. He had never been given that full report.

Back at WilmerHale, Ross learned that a member of his pro bono team was leaving to accept a new position, meaning he was about to lose a quarter of his workforce just as the already staggering workload on my case was growing even heavier. He went to the neighboring office of his friend and colleague, Shauna Friedman. "C'mon," Ross implored her, "how could you *not* want to be part of this?" Shauna knew that stepping up to join the team would mean sacrificing the precious little free time junior associates have to begin with. She and her husband, like Ross and his wife, were just shifting from the newlywed chapter of their lives into planning a family. She told Ross she would think about his offer overnight. The next morning, she agreed to come aboard.

With the new material in hand, Ross and Shauna began working on a brief to convince a judge there was enough evidence to exonerate me, or at least grant me a third trial. Why anything to do with the legal system is called a "brief," I'll never know, because such documents are anything but brief. By now, though, Ross was starting to get excited. He and his team had taken on my case determined to do everything they could to help me, but we were all well aware that finding anything new was a long shot thirty years after the crime. Ross's supervising partner, Peter Macdonald, had warned the lawyers early on not to get their hopes up. Righting an injustice only unfolds quickly and dramatically in the movies. In real life, trying to overturn a wrongful conviction is more often than not tedious, exhausting, and discouraging work, like putting a landslide back on top of the mountain with your bare hands, clearing the debris fistful by fistful. Learning that the prosecution had hidden evidence favorable to my defense could prove to be the game changer WilmerHale needed, though.

"We've got potential *Brady* material," Ross let Peter Macdonald know.

In 1963, in its landmark *Brady v. Maryland* decision, the U.S. Supreme Court ruled that it is a violation of a defendant's constitutional rights to due process for the prosecution to withhold any requested evidence favorable to the accused if that evidence is considered material either to guilt or to punishment. Whether the prosecutor acted in good faith and accidentally omitted the evidence, or willfully or maliciously did so, didn't matter as far as the court was concerned. Under today's *Brady* guidelines, prosecutors must automatically disclose any favorable evidence to the defense. If the D.A. or police had something such as a statement shooting down the credibility of one of their witnesses or piece of physical evidence that contradicted their theory of the crime, O'Neill was bound by law to share it with Mickey and his cocounsel, David Steinberg, before trial. Even evidence that doesn't point to innocence but could result in a lighter sentence has to be turned over. But that one word in the Supreme Court ruling—"material"—leaves a wide berth for interpretation by prosecutors, who often defend themselves against charges of *Brady* violations by arguing that the evidence they withheld was not "material" and would not, in fact, have enabled the defense, changed the verdict, or affected the sentencing. At best, it's still speculation: Who can really know except the jurors themselves what might have changed even a single crucial vote from guilty to innocent?

The similarities between the Crapser murder and the subsequent attack on the three King sisters had sent up a big red flag for the WilmerHale team from the get-go. First of all, both crimes were committed late at night against elderly white women in their homes just blocks apart. Emma Crapser and Mary King were asphyxiated by having cloth stuffed down their throats, and Catherine King, who survived, reported that her assailant had stuffed cloth and some kind of object into her mouth. The three King sisters and Emma Crapser were all bound and beaten in similar fashion. The attacks occurred within mere months of one another. Both apartments had been cased earlier in the day: Emma Crapser had expressed concern about the phony plumber whose description matched Donald Wise, while the Kings had accepted the Wise brothers' offer to shovel their snowy walkway earlier in the day and allowed them to come inside to warm up. Once inside, they had stolen a key to the apartment, which they used to gain access for the brutal crime later that night. Furthermore, both the King and Crapser attacks showed excessive violence—far beyond what it would take for a young man or teen to overpower an elderly woman in order to commit a robbery.

(That police suspected a link between the Crapser and King attacks was obvious, since they had immediately turned to their two main suspects in the unsolved Crapser case—me and Wayne Moseley. I was arrested and questioned in the King case two days after the murder, on February 22, 1978, but was immediately cut loose when my alibi checked out—I had been home sleeping. Moseley was asleep, too; police found him locked up in a state school for juvenile offenders. Next on the interrogation list were the Wise brothers. Anthony confessed that he, his brother Donald, and a guy named Saul Holland had carried out the King attack. Three sisters of Donald and Anthony, plus Anthony's girlfriend, Madeline Dixon South, also implicated the Wise boys.)

Even with all the new and previously undisclosed evidence in my favor, Ross knew that getting a judge to agree it merited a new trial would be a whole new courtroom battle with the D.A.'s office, one that could potentially drag on for months, if not years. Sending an innocent man to prison is far easier to do than undo, and I knew too well that O'Neill's arrogance and ambition would never allow him to admit he had made a terrible mistake, let alone try to right the wrong. He would fight this until he was on the ropes and couldn't get off.

I had already spent what by now amounted to half my life in prison for a crime I didn't commit, and Ross figured that the quickest way to free me would be to win parole. Since parole is generally determined by factors such as time served, rehabilitation, and accountability, citing new evidence and *Brady* violations was a long shot, but we had nothing else to lose. WilmerHale began putting together a fat portfolio to present to the parole board at what would be my fourth hearing. When they were done, there were 168 pages of documents supporting my release, bound together in a spiral book. There were copies of my diplomas and some of my fifty-plus certificates. There was also an eight-page report by an esteemed Harvard professor of psychiatry, Dr. James Beck, who concluded after two days of interviewing me that I wasn't a psychopath or antisocial, had above-average intelligence, and posed no threat of violence to the community. The doctor noted that I had made everything I possibly could of my life behind bars and was fully rehabilitated. I had been sober for twenty-three years and had become a man of deep faith. Plenty of people who had met me through the various programs I completed at Sing Sing went on record saying they were willing to give me a job when I got out.

Dr. Beck noted in particular what a strong impact a prison program by the Quakers on restorative justice had made on me. It's true: that program changed my whole perspective on crime. The program brought people who had been crime victims in to discuss what crime had done to their families. I remember this one young college coed came in to talk about the murder of her father. She didn't go into details about what had happened to him. She and her two brothers had been going to school, and the dad was the family's sole provider. When he died, all three kids had to quit school to take care of the household and help their mother. That really got to me. I had just never thought of the aftereffects of what I was doing when I was robbing and stealing and going around mugging people. What I might have done to that person's family, how my actions over the course of a minute or two could tear them down, had never entered my mind before. I did what I had to do, I survived, and that's it; it was in and gone and I didn't think about it anymore. But hearing this girl's thoughts and seeing her pain eye-to-eye, and hearing how it had taken away her education—that made me really look at life and the people I choose to be around me a lot differently. I had grown up knowing that I didn't matter to anyone, I didn't count. That my actions might have a profound effect on anyone else was honestly beyond my grasp. The girl who spoke to us that day in Restorative Justice helped me to see who I am and what I need to do as a human being to totally make sure that this never happened again with my life, that any impact I made was positive. Trena and Diamond spoke of my determination to make a positive contribution to society in their letters to the parole board, too. I also had letters of support from teachers, mentors, even prison officers. All of them put their own reputations on the line for me, vouching for my good character, and their belief in me kindled the smallest spark of hope as I stood in front of the board again in November 2008, praying that these strangers who never knew me would see I was a good man, ready to reenter society and live a peaceful and productive life with my wife and stepdaughter. I had written my own letter to the parole commissioners, as well, sharing my dreams of getting a job, providing for my family, and rebuilding myself in the eyes of a society that had written me off. I fantasized about going to the zoo, plays on Broadway, museums, the beach, an amusement park.

I expressed no remorse.

This time, Ross and his team tried to break the cycle of no-remorse-no-release by arguing that it unfairly put me in a catch-22 situation. It was impossible for me to meet the parole board's standards of demonstrating an appreciation for the nature and seriousness of the crime and show remorse when I had had nothing to do with it. It was like saying you can go to heaven only if you admit that you're Satan. I maintained my innocence consistently for over three decades, and never once changed my story even when a false confession could have spelled freedom. What the parole board needed to consider, WilmerHale suggested in a letter to the board, was that I was telling the truth, and to take measure of the lack of evidence, not the lack of remorse. "There have been, and likely will continue to be, instances in our criminal justice system where mistakes are made and people are wrongly convicted," my lawyers reminded them. "We urge the Board to consider that Mr. Bozella's claim of innocence has been correct all along, particularly in light of the new evidence that we have discovered during our investigation."

The parole board turned me down again but suggested the new evidence be used to petition the court for a new trial. Ross was planning to do that already, of course, but he took it as a good sign that the *Brady* violations were as obvious to someone else as they were to the WilmerHale team.

No matter how often I heard it, being denied parole still sucked the hope from me. What more could I do to prove myself? I had rebuilt my own character from whatever scraps of faith, hope, and charity I could scavenge behind prison walls, but it still wasn't enough. Trena overruled the latest rejection with her own fierce verdict.

"You're not getting out on parole, Dewey," she told me. "You're going to walk out a free man."

Not long after that, I found out that we'd gotten back onto the trailer rotation and called her with the happy news that we would get a conjugal visit in a matter of months. Trena laughed. "Well, we're not going to need it," she said. "You're going to be home by then. I know it." I let her keep hold of her happy-ending fantasy. I wanted to believe it, too.

A YEAR AFTER TAKING ON THE CASE AND ASKING THE D.A.'S OFFICE FOR ITS FILES, and only after filing a formal demand under the Freedom of Information Act, WilmerHale got a response from the D.A.'s office about our request for the case files in January of 2009. When they finally got permission to come copy certain files they'd requested, Ross and Shauna went up to Poughkeepsie to have a look. "Here you go," an assistant district attorney told them. They stared in disbelief. There were just two boxes from the Crapser murder, containing only material from the appeals, and nothing from the King case.

"There must be more," Shauna politely insisted. Grudgingly, the D.A.'s office produced a bunch of boxes on the King case, as well. The lawyers were given only a few hours to peruse and madly copy one page at a time. They eventually carted hundreds of pages of material back from Poughkeepsie. Sorting through their newly acquired files on the King murder, the WilmerHale team was stunned to come across a report about a *third* lookalike attack during that same time span and in the same area—a crime police had yet again linked to Donald Wise.

This one happened less than two months after the Crapser murder and six months before the King murder, when an eighty-two-year-old white woman named Estelle Dobler had been found severely beaten on her bedroom floor with her hands and legs bound. A stocking had been stuffed in her mouth, which was taped shut with black electrical tape. Ms. Dobler told police two black intruders had attacked her, one of them quite short. He matched the description of Donald Wise, who barely cleared five feet tall. Ross could find no record of any arrest or charges in the Dobler case, though, and there was no paper trail to suggest that police even bothered to go back to that case and reexamine it after they nailed the Wise brothers in the King case. Was there ever even a lineup after the King confessions to see if Estelle Dobler could identify the Wise brothers or Saul Holland? Not from what Ross and Shauna found.

Poughkeepsie police clearly knew that they had had three gruesomely similar cases in quick succession—Crapser, then Dobler, then King—with a confession and the survivors pointing toward Donald Wise, but investigators made no effort to put the pieces together. Instead, they sent the two Wises away for the King murder and called it a day. There were no similar attacks after they were locked up. So now the King case was solved, the Dobler case was being sidelined, and the Crapser case remained open.

Five years had passed, remember, since the time the first grand jury refused to indict me right after the murder and my arrest. Five years that O'Neill and his minions had had to dig up anything corroborating Lamar Smith's story about seeing me and Wayne Moseley break into 15 North Hamilton that night, but still they had none. What they did have was mounting evidence that I *didn't* do it, but once they had decided to lock in on me as the scapegoat in the Crapser slaying, they weren't going to look elsewhere. The evidence in my favor, the district attorney's office determined, was best kept secret or destroyed.

The disturbing revelations kept coming as the WilmerHale team continued to plow through the mountain of newly released D.A. files.

My attorneys could see that the only reason the Dobler report was even tucked into the King file was because Donald Wise had, in fact, been considered a prime suspect in the Dobler attack, though no one appears to have ever been indicted or charged. Less than a month after the Dobler attack, Art Regula and a fellow detective,

Enno Groth, with the knowledge of Assistant D.A. Otto Williams, had interviewed a friend of the Wise brothers at police headquarters. Christopher Gill lived in the same apartment building as Mrs. Dobler, and he told detectives that Donald Wise had been at his place until eleven thirty that night. Gill reported that Wise stayed behind in the building after Gill went out. He also said Wise had made some reference to Mrs. Dobler, but when pressed for details, Gill clammed up. Police records also showed that investigators had compared the Dobler and King crimes while building their King case to show that Wise used the same modus operandi more than once, and his crimes bore a telling signature in the gruesome way the elderly women were savagely beaten, bound, and suffocated. But the homicide detectives' basic connect-the-dots skills were either very, very bad or very, very shady, because the link between the Dobler and Crapser cases was even clearer than the link between Dobler and King: not only was the modus operandi similar, but Donald Wise's fingerprint was right there on Ms. Crapser's bathroom window (even though investigators didn't bother to process it for five years, until right before my first trial in 1983). So why was the Dobler report kept out of the Crapser file, and never disclosed? Because, the D.A. argued when WilmerHale demanded an answer, they didn't consider any of this "favorable."

Also squirreled away inside the district attorney's file of the King murder was a cassette tape from a Poughkeepsie police interview of Saul Holland on January 23, 1978. No one on the prosecution side had mentioned this telling piece of evidence in my favor for thirty-one years, either. Holland was the Wises' accomplice in the King attack, and the police recorded an interview with him just one day after a Poughkeepsie newspaper had quoted the district attorney himself saying that law enforcement officials saw a possible "parallel" between the King and Crapser murders. The WilmerHale team asked the D.A. for a copy of the tape.

When Shauna read the transcript on a Saturday night, she couldn't believe her eyes: here was Saul Holland telling Assistant D.A. William O'Neill and two arresting detectives that Donald Wise had boasted of having committed a similar crime and getting away with it before the King murder.

"Oh, they had did—they had did one of these jobs here before," Holland said, adding that Donald Wise had assured him "you ain't got nothing to be scared of or nervous about." Holland then described what Wise had told him about the previous crime.

"He said the way they did it, they, you know, when they got to the house, there wasn't nobody there, you know, and they just found all this money and stuff and then around 9 or 10 or 11, that's when the lady came home. She must have come home."

His interrogators cut him off before he could go on.

Holland's recorded statement had been taken only after O'Neill and the two cops had conducted a preliminary interview; listening back to the taped version, Ross and Shauna could tell that this wasn't the first time investigators had discussed this with Holland, and that they were keen to keep him focused only on the King murder once they hit the record button. There was no unsolved crime in Poughkeepsie other than the Crapser murder that could remotely fit the description Holland had just given of an earlier Wise attack, yet none of the three investigators expressed any surprise or even interest in the major lead Holland had just dropped in their laps. Just the opposite: one of the cops, Officer William Grey, hastily interrupted Holland to try to get him to go back on script.

"Well, I don't want to get into that because we're liable to get confused," he redirected Holland when Holland mentioned the previous Wise burglary where the old woman had come home. They didn't bother to ask him (or, it seems, the Wise brothers) anything more about the mystery attack that matched the Crapser case right down to what was stolen, and they were either too dim, too lazy, or too determined to pin the murder on me to have the fingerprint from Emma Crapser's bathroom window immediately tested against the latent prints they had on file for Donald Wise. Hell, for that matter, if they had investigated Ms. Crapser's murder right, they could have matched that print to Donald Wise and zeroed in on him from the beginning.

Then Mary King's life wouldn't have been taken.

And mine wouldn't have been, either.

When Ross attempted to find Saul Holland to interview him for himself, he discovered that Holland had been left mentally incapacitated after being tased by police in a confrontation that resulted in a civil rights lawsuit over excessive force. The tape and transcript would have to do.

With the neighbors' statements about the undamaged door, the empty street, and the banging trash can in the alley; the Dobler report; and the Holland tape, my lawyers had found not just one *Brady* violation, but several. The WilmerHale investigation had also led to a new witness, a woman named Terri Holman. Ms. Holman recalled several conversations with Madeline Dixon South and two other women about the murder of Emma Crapser. Ms. Holman, who had been dating Madeline's brother, recalled Madeline telling her how Donald Wise had cased the Crapser apartment by posing as a plumber earlier in the day, and he killed Ms. Crapser because she recognized him when she interrupted his burglary later that night. During my first trial, Madeline Dixon South had testified that Donald and her then-boyfriend Anthony Wise had left her

house the night of the Crapser murder, returned later with jewelry, then walked her past 15 North Hamilton the next morning
and said it was where their "movie" had taken place. Madeline had
passed away before my second trial, but Terri Holman now told my
legal team that Madeline had picked through the stolen jewelry and
dumped costume pieces into a nearby creek.

IN APRIL 2009, WILMERHALE FILED A MOTION IN DUTCHESS COUNTY COURT for my
conviction to be overturned on grounds of new evidence, actual
innocence, and the violation of my constitutional right to due process through the D.A.'s withholding of *Brady* material.

Between two murder trials, every possible appeal, and the cru-
sades led first by the Innocence Project and now by WilmerHale, my
entire adult life had hinged on legal motions. I had long since lost
count of how many there had been. But this one, I knew, wasn't
just another motion.

This was my last chance to prove I did not kill Emma Crapser.

12

HOPE **IS A CHEAP WORD, TOO FLIMSY TO HOLD ITS OWN WEIGHT.** Tell me why we have so many words to capture every little variation of the color blue, but none for the hundred different shades of hope? There should be separate words for the hope of a college kid on graduation day and the hope of a cancer patient being wheeled into the operating room. There should be an easy way to explain the profound difference between having hope and dwelling inside it, between Christmas Eve and a murder trial. For twenty-six years, I had made hope my safe haven within hell. I knew that to stop believing was to stop being. I had seen what could happen to men who couldn't sustain that illusion, to a human being who could no longer find even an inch of "maybe" to hold on to. I'll never forget a single week during the holidays in 1995, when there were five suicides inside the walls of Sing Sing, one after the other. Four were hangings—one over a woman, another to escape homosexual violence—and one was a white guy who cut both wrists and bled out. Everyone just thought he was sleeping until someone finally noticed the blood pooled under his cot. That same depressing week, another white guy bugged out and cut off his penis and tried to pull out one of his eyes. He survived, though.

I wasn't a total stranger to suicidal despair myself: I had once hit rock bottom when I was locked up in Poughkeepsie early on. It's not something I ever talk about. Conditioning myself to be optimistic, to hold on to a positive attitude, took time and perseverance, but my mind had developed the muscle it needed to keep a firm grip. Still, I couldn't help but wonder how much hope I would have left if WilmerHale lost this final push for my freedom. I told myself not to let my mind go there, to just wait and pray and see what God's plan was, but that was tough. Ross had warned that we could be in for a wait. First of all, District Attorney William Grady would have to file his formal response to our allegations that his office had suppressed evidence. But aside from a canned quote in the local paper from Grady, who said he intended to conduct a thorough investigation into the alleged *Brady* violations, there was nothing but the sound of crickets chirping from Poughkeepsie. When Ross called to ask about the delay, no one would take his calls or return his messages. As we waited, the judge assigned to the case recused himself because it turned out he had been an attorney in the D.A.'s office at the time of the Crapser murder. Another county superior court justice took over, and this one finally lost patience when the D.A.'s office blew off filing deadlines and wouldn't return calls from the judge's clerk. After nearly six weeks of stonewalling, the D.A. eventually responded to a written reprimand and stern warning from the second judge and filed his papers in early July.

The second judge retired at the end of August.

The third judge, the Honorable James T. Rooney, was actually from neighboring Putnam County, which Ross considered a welcome bit of good news, since Dutchess County had proven to be what lawyers term a "hostile venue" for me for thirty years. Judge Rooney would review the documents from both sides and decide whether to hold a hearing on the merits of our case or to just issue his ruling. Ross was confident that the prosecution's own records clearly proved that my constitutional rights had been violated, but he was always careful to hedge his bets whenever I asked what our chances were of getting a new trial, let alone an acquittal. When Ross and Shauna Friedman came up for a visit during our six-month wait, Ross's boss, Peter Macdonald, tagged along. I tried to sound casual when I put the same question to him.

"So what do you think our odds are?" I asked.

"Ninety percent," he quickly replied. Ross and Shauna exchanged a worried look. It's not like I started jumping up and down and clapping my hands or anything, but virtually promising victory to a client—much less one who's been waiting half his lifetime for justice—was a bold thing to do. The added pressure from their managing partner was probably the last thing they needed at that point, since I was their first criminal case, and neither Ross nor Shauna had made their courtroom debut as a lawyer yet. WilmerHale had already spent more than $1 million on my case, and the investment was as personal as it was professional—Ross drafted part of the brief working eight hours a day on a Caribbean vacation, and Shauna had sacrificed a lot of time with her family, too. I knew those were hours and days and weeks they'd never get back. They had to be anxious and exhausted, but they never complained. Winning this case would be a major victory for them as well as for me. I nodded and tried to let Peter's prediction soak in. This could be it.

Spring turned to summer and summer to fall. Still no word from the judge. Trena came to visit one afternoon and asked me to do her a favor.

"Dewey, I want you to start giving away your clothes and things," she said. "You're coming out of here. I know you are."

We'd been together for more than a decade and had been through some wrenching times, and I knew better than to question Trena's intuition by then. I started doling out my belongings to my fellow inmates. Like Santa convicted Claus, I handed out socks, long johns, sneakers, all my extra sweats, pants, and shirts. If Trena was wrong, it was going to be one cold-ass winter.

ON OCTOBER 14, 2009, A FRIDAY AFTERNOON, ROSS GOT A CALL from a reporter at the *Poughkeepsie Journal.*

"I hear congrats are in order," the journalist began.

"What are you talking about?" Ross asked.

"I just got off the phone with the D.A. I heard your motion was granted."

Ross jumped off the line and dialed Judge Rooney's chambers. The clerk confirmed that the judge had rendered his opinion.

"It's in the mail," she said.

"Can you please e-mail or fax it to me?" Ross cajoled.

"We don't do that," the clerk answered. Ross turned the charm up full blast, and she finally caved. He scanned the first page as soon as it arrived, but the decision wasn't there, and not on the next page or in the next ten pages, either. He flipped ahead until he found what he was looking for, on page 49.

"It is hereby ORDERED that the motion is granted to the extent that the judgment of conviction of the defendant for Murder in the Second Degree is vacated and a new trial is ordered."

A hearing was scheduled for October 28, 2009, for "further proceedings."

Shauna was at a wedding in Newport, Rhode Island, and couldn't be reached, and Peter wasn't in his office. Ross picked up the phone, eager to share the good news with someone.

"Trena, are you sitting down?"

"Oh my God."

"Yeah, we won!"

Trena let out a scream so loud and long that Ross later described it as the rawest human emotion he had ever witnessed. Finally, she caught her breath.

"Sorry!"

"I'm here. You do whatever you have to do."

The next day, Trena came to visit. We hugged and kissed, then sat down.

"Dewey, I got something to tell you," Trena began. I braced myself for some kind of bad news—my default setting.

"Dewey, your case has been overturned."

I stared at her in disbelief, unable to even process the happy news.

"Stop kidding, stop playing!" I finally said.

"I'm not," Trena replied. The smile on her face assured me this was real, and a thousand and more things shot through my mind at once. I hollered for everyone to hear.

"My case has been overturned!!"

All the inmates, visitors, and COs within hearing distance offered their congratulations. *Really? Really? Good for you!*

I knew too well that all I could do now was pray.

On Sunday, Ross, Shauna, and Trena arranged a conference call to phone me with more details. If there was going to be a third trial, Ross promised, he would at least try to get me out on bail for the duration.

I had a million questions—How much would bail be, and how

could we ever afford it? How long would we have to wait for the third trial? What about all the evidence that had been destroyed? No one had any answers yet, though, and all I could do was hang tight. I felt strangely calm, as if showing how desperately I wanted my freedom would chase it away again. "I'm not going to blow this," I promised the WilmerHale team by way of thanks. "If I get out, I'm going to make you proud."

Things were still up in the air until the hearing in two weeks. While Judge Rooney had found the law and facts supporting our charges that prosecutors had suppressed evidence "compelling" and "indeed overwhelming," he had refused to speculate about my actual guilt or innocence. He did find the similarities "striking" between the Crapser, Dobler, and King assaults. "In addition to the advanced age of the victims, the proximity of the crimes in time and location and information connecting Donald Wise to all three assaults, the perpetrators tried to or did stuff material down the victims' throats," he noted, adding that the killers had also talked their way inside both the King and Crapser homes earlier in the day to case the apartments. If the jury had been given the evidence that Donald Wise was involved in two other alarmingly similar attacks on elderly women, Judge Rooney said, there was a "reasonable possibility" that I would have been acquitted. Referring to Lamar Smith and Wayne Moseley's finger-pointing, he also pointed out that the only evidence connecting me to the crime "was the testimony of two extremely interested witnesses with serious credibility problems, who were admittedly using mind altering substances."

That said, Judge Rooney did not reprimand the prosecution for any misconduct and explained that he did not think they had acted in bad faith or had intentionally skirted the law. We now had to wait and see what the district attorney's office planned to do next. My guilty verdict had been vacated once before in 1990, when the court had agreed my first trial was unfair because prosecutors had excluded African Americans from the jury, but my second trial wrongfully convicted me for a second time. There was no guarantee a third trial wouldn't end the same way, even with all the new *Brady* evidence we had discovered. Juries are unpredictable. I will live my life by the law until the day I die, but I will never again trust the law.

WHEN OCTOBER 28 CAME AROUND, I FELT EXCITED AND TENSE, like I was waiting to go into the ring against a titleholder. My head throbbed. Shauna arrived at the county jail where I was being held to keep me company before the deputies came to transport me to the courthouse. Ross had already gone on ahead to settle in at the defense table. Shauna produced a dark suit, white shirt, and red tie some paralegal had picked out for me to wear for my big day, and I thanked her while cringing at the junior banker's sense of style.

"I look like Ross," I observed with some alarm. Joking did nothing to relieve the stress. Perspiration was beading on my face, and I felt sick with anxiety. "This is the worst headache I've ever had," I told Shauna. She gave me a hug before leaving.

"There's a good chance you're going to get out today," she said. "We'll see you in the courtroom."

Ross had tried to connect with the D.A.'s office to find out how they planned to move forward, but as usual, no one gave him the courtesy of a return call. None of us knew what to expect that morning, but the national media was waiting for us in Poughkeepsie. Both the *New York Times* and CBS News had sent reporters.

I saw TV crews and heard the whir of cameras as I entered the courtroom in my new suit and shackles. I took my seat next to Ross and Shauna at the defense table, the chains around my waist and ankles clanking. Ross had never seen me cuffed and chained before, and the sight must have unnerved him. He patted my back. Trena and Diamond sat behind us, smiling nervously in their Sunday best. Judge Rooney called the court to order and summarized the reason for the hearing, then asked the assistant district attorney, Edward Whitesell, how the prosecution planned to proceed. Whitesell peered down through his glasses to read a long statement. I couldn't interpret the legal mumbo jumbo over the thump of my heart and the rush of blood in my ears. I heard someone mention that many of the original witnesses were no longer available and that the indictment was dismissed. Before it could register, I heard Judge Rooney's voice, strong and clear.

"Mr. Bozella is ordered to be released immediately."

The guards stepped up and unlocked my shackles, and I sat for a moment, shaking my head in dazed silence before the tears began to roll down my cheeks and I stood up, a free man. Trena rushed into my arms and we held each other tight, kissing and crying. *It's over,* I whispered to her, *it's over.*

13

THE FIRST AFTERSHOCK HIT ON THE RIDE HOME. I settled into Ross's front seat for a quick trip back to the county jail to pick up my few belongings before catching up with Trena back at the apartment for the home-coming party she was busy throwing together. I still couldn't quite believe the whole miracle of what had just happened. I felt like an actor who needed to absorb the story before he could feel the character. I stared at Ross's dashboard. The lights, the video displays, the buttons . . . cars hadn't looked like that in the '80s, the last time I rode in a front seat. As Ross pulled out, a clipped voice out of nowhere began giving directions. Thing didn't know shit about the streets of Poughkeepsie. I started arguing with it.

"It's a GPS," Ross explained. Some satellite in the sky tracking us on the ground, with a computer telling us where we were and how to get where we were going. Straight out of sci-fi.

"Damn," I said, then: "It's all wrong, man, you need to take this next left, then—"

"I think," Ross cut me off with a laugh, "that I'm better off fol-lowing the directions *not* coming from a guy who's spent the last twenty-six years locked up."

He turned out to be right, though it would take me a while to admit it even to myself: I didn't know my way around the real world anymore, and me learning how to navigate it was going to be a rough ride for everyone.

Sing Sing owed me forty dollars from my commissary account, but I had no intention of picking it up. I could have used the money, but the cost of going back there to ask for it was too high for me. After all the years I did, they had even taken my pants, boots, and shirt before sending me in prison greens to the county jail to await the hearing that resulted in my release. Poughkeepsie had swapped Sing Sing's greens for their own orange jumpsuit, and at the end of the day, I was put out on the streets a free man with not a dime or stitch of clothing to my name. Just the suit WilmerHale had bought me.

Back at Trena's place—now our place—a small welcoming party of friends, supporters, and lawyers celebrated my homecoming with pizza, grilled chicken, and soda. The first game of the World Series was on TV, with the Phillies defending their title against the Yankees at Yankee Stadium. At Sing Sing, a major sports event usually spelled trouble of some sort on the blocks—careless trash talking, an unpaid gambling debt, a shiv between the ribs—and you had to pay more attention to what was happening around you than to the game itself. The risk wasn't worth the effort, and I tended to stay away from those rec periods. My first night of freedom was cool and misty, but our one-bedroom apartment was warm and full of good cheer, good food, good people. Trena couldn't stop smiling. Diamond hung in the background, shy and uncertain. In pictures from that day, I look happy but a little dazed, the victorious boxer whose ears are still ringing from a powerful head shot. "So what's next?" everybody wanted to know. There was a long, long list in my mind that I was meaning to write down and ponder through a wide-open lens of possibility. I knew that more than any degree I had earned, I had to count on the self-help curriculum I'd designed for myself in prison. All the advice I had carefully copied into the notebooks I'd kept in my cell for so many years was finally going to get put to the test. The most important lessons were committed to memory, and I recited them to myself like a mantra.

Fear. Fear kills dreams. I could not open my door to fear, not even a crack, or it would come crashing in like a tidal wave and drown me.

Commitment. Once you step in the ring, you see the fight through, even if you're outmatched. Pain isn't what defeats you; not giving a shit does.

Persistence. In all things you do. It's not how much weight you can lift that proves your strength; it's how many reps you can do. Repetition builds muscle and muscle memory, not just with your body, but with your character, as well.

Hope and faith. Without this, it's impossible to overcome struggle and conflict, which every human being faces in one way or another. I wasted a lot of precious time in my life before I believed in God and understood that he had a plan for me, that I had to trust there was a purpose to my suffering.

Forgiveness. Anger and frustration are death by slow poison. If you don't forgive, you can't move forward. It's that simple. And that hard.

Once the guests had cleared out of our one-bedroom apartment, I fell asleep on the floor next to the bed Trena and Diamond had always shared. I woke with every sound through the night—the neighbor's key unlocking the door, the wind rustling dead leaves outside, a car alarm three blocks over. My body heard everything before I did, and my muscles would already be taut each time my eyes flew open. I was still in prison. Still on point. In the morning, I got up early and found a small saucepan to boil water for my coffee. Trena joined me at the kitchen's rickety table to figure out some answers to that question still hanging stale in yesterday's party air. What next?

A job was the obvious answer, and the most urgent task at hand. Trena and Diamond had been teetering on the edge of homelessness, getting by on Diamond's $1,100 monthly paycheck from McDonald's while waiting for a red-tape mess over Trena's disability check to get untangled. I was eager to start providing for my family. I snatched up the first job I could and went to work part-time at the local Walmart, stacking boxes and cleaning shelves for $8.50 an hour. It was just temporary work for a couple of weeks during the holidays. I started on Black Friday, working back in the TV department. Gotta hand it to Walmart: hiring a dude with experience in prison riots was a helluva smart move. People were going nuts. I did exactly what I used to do in the prison yard—kept my eyes open, my back to the wall, and minded my own business. The big difference was how much I enjoyed the chaos this time around. Just being surrounded by all different kinds of people, in all different kinds of clothes, soaking in all the new color, the new sounds, I felt alive in a way I never had before. My senses were on overload.

Even after my Walmart job was over, I found myself seeking out places where I could be by myself inside a crowd. I happily discovered that the role I had perfected in prison, the detached observer, translated to the outside world as a form of entertainment instead of survival. The Poughkeepsie mall became my favorite hangout, an easy bus ride from home. Going there turned into a daily ritual. Even if I had only a little spending money, I would buy something small—usually a movie or CD—just for that buzz of gratification I got from being able to choose, from doing something so completely ordinary. Fun had become a lost concept to me. The word itself seemed alien, from a foreign language I had once known but forgotten. *Fun* hadn't crossed my mind, much less my lips, for twenty-six years. Even being able to idly browse through the stores for hours and ponder my choices was satisfying. I tried on a pair of ostrich boots and promised myself a pair someday. I bought Trena my first gift not from a prison commissary—a ring with little diamonds in it at Kay Jewelers.

My first day in the mall, I parked myself in the middle of the food court to people-watch. I had to get used to regular people again. I was happy, hell yes, I was happy, but the numbness was slow to wear off, and I needed to discover what feelings actually *felt* like again. I wanted to scoop up the world in greedy handfuls and bury my face in the sweetness of it, but I was paralyzed, frozen in place. I would get my greasy Chinese food and choose a table where I could sit with my back against the wall and clear sight lines in front and beside me. I watched shoppers stream past and felt calmed by the white noise of their chatter and laughter, the parents scolding runaway toddlers, the teenagers showing off, the old men griping at wives who ignored them. It all washed over me, until the afternoon I heard an unfamiliar sound, one that pierced me straight through.

How long had it been since I had heard a baby crying? I felt something give inside me, a soft collapse.

That's when I knew I was home.

That one baby's cry gave me a rush of joy that no street drug ever could, back in the day. Why is it that people always want to hush their children? Every day, I would go to the mall and listen for those few bars of lost music. *Let them cry!* I mentally urged every passing parent who shushed their squalling baby. *Please let me hear that beautiful sound!*

THE DAY THAT I SAT DOWN WITHOUT THINKING at a table in the middle of the food court, my back exposed to the tables full of strangers behind me, I busted out laughing. *I'm free!* I thought as I started eating. *I'm finally free. Fucking free.* Six months, it had taken, just to sink in.

I lined up a position as a counselor at a nonprofit organization that helped parolees reestablish themselves back in society, placing them in jobs or training programs, putting them on track to complete their educations if they'd dropped out. The job wasn't going to pay the bills, but I liked it, especially when I got through to some young knucklehead the way Shariff had reached me so many years ago in the prison yard. My old mentor had passed, but the lessons he taught me had held true no matter how my life twisted and turned over the years.

Some of the parolees I coached got serious about themselves and their futures; they were the ones who landed factory jobs and ended up making fifteen, sixteen dollars an hour. Others didn't get it, and maybe never would. I had one kid who thought he had it all figured out, that he could just keep hanging out on the streets and play like he was the man. He wouldn't follow through on any attempts to line him up with a legitimate job or secure a spot in a program that would give him a marketable skill. I was more determined than he was to turn his life around. I went by his house to try to talk sense into him, but he was full of attitude. I noticed scars on his face and body; it looked like he'd gotten into a fight.

"Yo, man, what happened?" I asked. "Code of the streets, man," he replied, puffed up with his own self-importance. When I went by a second time, he wouldn't even come to the door. I called him on the phone, instead. We talked for maybe a minute before he hung up. *You'll need me,* I said to myself. It was his mother I heard from next, begging me to do something.

"My son is in lockup," she said.

"Really? What for?" I asked.

"Possession of a gun."

I told her it was out of my hands now.

Live with the consequences, homie, I silently said. *You wanna be a thug, deal with your time. Handle it. You thought you were a man, but you're not. Listen to the brothers trying to save you that kind of hurt.*

Trena thought I needed counseling myself, that I couldn't just walk out of prison after twenty-six years for a murder I didn't commit and plug right into real life. I thought I was doing okay, myself. Handling it. I had my dreams for a future, and it seemed like the big pieces were coming together, but lots of little pieces were missing. It was like getting the best present imaginable on Christmas morning but then discovering the instructions on how to put it together were missing. I knew how to make french fries in a prison cell without a deep fryer, but doing a load of laundry blew my mind.

"I lost a sock," Trena announced one day as she came in from the Laundromat with a load of my freshly washed clothes.

"What do you mean?" I asked.

"Disappeared," she said with a shrug. "Only one of them came out."

I shook my head, disbelieving. Where was my white tube sock? This made no sense.

"How the hell can you lose a sock in the laundry?" I bellowed. "It's impossible!"

Trena was taken aback by my genuine outrage.

"It happens, Dewey. Why are you getting so worked up over a sock? There's war going on, people are dying in Iraq and Afghanistan—" she started in. I cut her off.

"By the way, it's *my* sock, not your sock. Why wasn't it your damn sock?"

Trena looked at me and spoke firmly, trying to get through a wall whose thickness she couldn't fathom.

"Dewey, you can buy new socks now," she said at last.

My clothes were important to me. Overly important, she would say. I had to have them all in a certain order that only I understood. Trena would put them away, and I would hover anxiously, then slip back into the bedroom later to sort and rearrange it all. Trena finally gave up trying to figure out my system and just left the laundry basket in the bedroom for me to take care of. She couldn't understand why my socks, my pants, even my sneakers, were of such vital interest. They were my things, that was why. In prison, you are only issued so many socks a year. If you want to keep them, you never send them to the prison laundry; you pay someone who works in the laundry to do yours separately. My socks never got lost in Sing Sing.

Fugitive socks weren't the only thing that baffled me. It fell on Trena to walk me through the mundane steps of day-to-day life, like filling out job applications on a computer, or getting health insurance, or filing taxes. I had little patience for the niggling details and rigid reality of things like a computer program automatically rejecting me as a job candidate because I had a record. If a recruiter would just meet me face-to-face, I knew they would see how serious

I was and give me a chance, but I didn't know how to negotiate the ever-changing obstacle course of the outside world, and I hated any confrontation. Confrontation, from my vantage point of the past three decades, anyway, was almost always explosive. I knew how to keep my head down and avoid a shank between the ribs, but I had no skills when it came to arguing with the cable company. Trena always knew when to push and how hard. It was easier to withdraw and let her deal with the frustrating things for me. She was fight; I was flight. I was too caught up in my own world to notice the resentment building inside her.

The outside world was constantly bombarding me with new or rediscovered things to see and hear, taste and touch. Just being able to choose for myself—whether it was what kind of bread for my sandwich at the deli or what time to go to bed at night—felt so damn good that I sometimes went overboard. Every morning, I would go to the quick-shop to buy lottery tickets and sugary treats to indulge my sweet tooth—Little Debbie cakes, candy bars, soda—I couldn't decide, so I bought them all. *Damn candy bar costing a dollar twenty-five, a soda two bucks, what the fuck is this?* I thought. Life is a lot more expensive when you're not bartering for everything with loose cigarettes. I'd come home and empty that little sack like some king piling up his gold to admire. I'd scratch off my lottery tickets, never disappointed that I hadn't won an instant million dollars or fifty thousand or even five, but happy that I'd had the chance. Trena and I would have coffee together, and she would just shake her head at the ritual I had to follow to make it, boiling my water in my favorite pan on the back left burner. If she or Diamond moved the pan to another burner, it irritated me and I would move it back. I suppose the psychiatrist I refused to see would say that was a symptom of institutionalization, that I took comfort in the predictability of small things I could control. What I didn't understand was why it should matter to anyone how I made my damn coffee.

That newfound greediness about making choices and wanting to feel in control led to my first big postrelease blowup with Trena. I honestly thought I was doing something good for the both of us, that this was how you went about being the head of household: I bought a new sofa. With three of us living in the apartment now, and some money saved away, it was time to upgrade from Trena's smaller, worn-out couch to something the whole family could lounge around on. Trena and I had decided the week before to shop for a new one. So I went to the furniture store and chose a big, deep sofa in black leather. I brushed off the saleswoman who wondered whether I might want to check with my wife before ordering it.

Trena was furious. She was convinced I did it because we'd just had some squabble and I'd gotten worked up and wanted to prove myself. "You wanted to be Mr. Big Shot," she fumed. We kept the couch, but it remained a hot button for her, and literally a sore spot for me: I can't sit on it for long. After a lifetime on hard surfaces, my body can't deal with softness.

Both Trena and Diamond felt disrupted by my sudden presence in what had been their snug mother-daughter space for so long. No one had had time to gradually adapt—I wasn't a date who became a boyfriend who became an occasional overnight guest before moving in and then marrying Trena. I was an absentee husband and stepfather of more than a decade who arrived out of nowhere and started taking up space—emotionally and physically—that hadn't been cleared for me yet. "Dewey, you've been in the bathroom for an hour and ten minutes!" I would hear Trena complain outside the door as I used up all the hot water and fresh towels, enjoying the luxury of taking a shower whenever I wanted and for as long as I wanted, conveniently forgetting there was only one bathroom in the house with two women waiting for their turns to use it.

Diamond and I weren't communicating much at all. Reserved by nature, she had withdrawn even more around me. As Trena struggled with poor health over the past several years, Diamond had become the rock she leaned on. I knew my stepdaughter felt like I was invading her territory—I was, after all—but I trusted that she would come back around if I gave her space. Trena kept trying to force it, though, nagging Diamond to socialize if we were sitting in the kitchen and she came in after work to grab a snack. "Why aren't you talking?" she barked at her one night. Diamond angrily bolted out the door. I went looking for her; it bothered the shit out of me that I couldn't find her, but she came back on her own a half hour later.

"I promised your father I wouldn't let nothing happen to you, that I'd take care of you," I reminded her. Trena's ex and I had a civil relationship, and I respected his place in Diamond's life. "You can't be doing this shit like running away! This is not how I want this to be!" Diamond confirmed that she felt displaced and resented how I was always using all the hot water or bogarting the TV. It hurt my feelings, but I needed to hear it. Even before I went to prison, I had never known what it was like to be part of a normal family. All I could do was learn as I went, and that process wasn't as smooth or easy as any of us had hoped.

This wasn't anything like my fantasy of coming home from a white-collar job in a nice suit, putting my own key in my own front door, walking into a house I'd bought for my family to find them waiting eagerly for me, the smells of dinner cooking on the stove wafting in from the kitchen. This was hard and frustrating. I never expected freedom to be such hard work. I was different. Even the way I sat and contemplated things alarmed Trena. "It's not normal to stare at a wall for hours!" she objected, not understanding that a blank wall, in prison, is your mind's only canvas. Other times, I would spend all afternoon playing chess with the computer, addicted as much if not more to the offer, always, of another chance, as I was to the game itself. Chess reminded me a lot of boxing.

Even the lighter moments between Trena and me carried reminders of where I had been and what I had gone through. My default setting was a prison yard. My body often automatically processed as a threat whatever I didn't expect. One time, Trena was feeling playful and decided to creep into the bedroom and scare me like she was a monster. I almost took her head off. "Don't ever sneak up on me!" I yelled. Truthfully, she didn't scare me nearly as much as my own reaction did. Self-defense is a habit. The edge I had honed so carefully in Sing Sing seems to be a permanent part of me now; I can't just undo it or flip a switch to turn my hyperawareness off for good. And I'm not so sure I would want to, anyway. I know better than most people that anything can happen in this world.

AFTER SEVEN MONTHS IN MY PAROLEE COUNSELING JOB, I knew it was time to move on to the next level. I needed a better paycheck, for one thing. But I couldn't bring myself to say I was quitting—it felt like I was abandoning people who needed me—and Trena ended up calling in to quit for me. I took comfort in the other volunteer outlet I had, which I hoped would be the warm-up exercise toward realizing my biggest dream, of owning my own gym and running a boxing program to keep at-risk kids off the streets. An old friend of mine named Ray had a gym in Newburgh, and a couple of aspiring young boxers were training there. I helped out around the gym and coached the kids who sought me out.

Sometimes my ingrained prison ways drove Trena crazy, like the way I would just plow forward, looking straight ahead, without noticing if I was cutting in front of people. I had to consciously remind myself where I was. I was used to looking out just for myself, but the very skill that had saved me was dogging me now.

"You know, Dewey, it's not about you no more," Trena said more than once.

Now and then her patience wore thin, especially when there was some ordinary problem with a reservation, or tickets, or what have you, and I reverted to my "avoid confrontation" mode and made Trena deal with it alone. Shutting out everything and everyone around me used to keep me untouchable; now it made me unreachable to those who cared about me most. Trena kept pushing for me to get counseling, first for myself, and later, as a couple, but I have zero interest in sitting around talking to some stranger who can never understand where I'm coming from. I've lost too much time to waste more. I am who I am, the way I am.

I came to recognize that certain things never failed to agitate me, and I would have to make a conscious effort to work on my attitude. For starters, I couldn't stand people telling me what to do. I read too much into harmless requests that sounded, through ears accustomed to little else, like orders. *You better do this* or *You have to* are casual words that a loving wife says, but the ex-inmate hears, and taking out the trash suddenly isn't about a household chore anymore. *I ain't doing nothin' period.* I had to learn how not to let my ego, my pride, get in the way. I made myself come back to apologize, because I was wrong. But Trena and I sometimes felt locked in position, caught out time and again in these small storms that rolled through our marriage.

TENSIONS IN OUR SMALL FAMILY RELAXED once we were able to afford a two-bedroom, two-bath apartment in the same complex. Diamond got her own room and her own TV, and one day brought home a Yorkshire terrier pup whose antics could instantly take the edge off any bad day. The bigger issues still shadowed us, though, and Trena started seeing a marriage counselor without me. I wasn't going to be bullied into going. Some differences, I reasoned, were just the way we are, and we needed to let them be and move on. Charity was one of those ongoing debates.

If I see a need and I can do something about it, I'll act impulsively. At the gas station, there was a guy with a sign in his hand one day. I didn't know if he wanted the money for drugs, but I didn't care. My thing is, I follow my heart. I watched him take the cash I gave him and go inside and buy some soup. Another time, I was standing in line at the dollar store behind a lady and her little girl as they unloaded their cart full of clothes and cheap toys. The woman went to pay, and the clerk said her credit card had been declined. The little girl and her mother started putting everything back in the cart, and I could see the girl's face, the hurt she was trying not to show.

"Nah, put it back up there," I told them. The mother looked up at me. "Don't worry about it. It's from me to you. You and your daughter." I gave the cashier ninety dollars in cash. "What'd you do that for?" the clerk asked me as the grateful mother and daughter carried their bags out the door. I just shrugged. "Because I could."

Trena has deep compassion, but she is ruled more by reason than emotion. The crack addicts at church showed us how differently we regard an outstretched hand.

We were sitting there before services one Sunday when a young woman came up to us and grabbed hold of Trena's arm. They'd exchanged pleasantries on previous occasions, and now the woman told her, "I don't have any money and I need some shoes. Can you help me with some shoes?" Trena handed her some bills with a gentle warning: "If I see you come into church and you don't have on the shoes I bought you, we have trouble."

Another girl approached me directly, in her tight torn jeans and skimpy top. "Mmmm, you fine," she crooned. "Can you help me with a dollar, or two dollars?" Trena came up, blood in her eye. The hooker tried to win her over. "Ma'am, I'm so sorry I disrespected you." I was digging out my wallet. Trena shot me a look.

"Don't give it to her," she said. "Wake up."

I gave the girl some money.

The next time we saw her, she was marching through the aisles of the church with a crack pipe in her mouth, sucking on it, slurring, "Anybody help me with this pipe? I need some crack. I want some crack." Trena turned on me.

"Now do you understand? When you're giving this young lady money, you understand that your blood is on her body? If she overdoses or gets killed by some dealer, you helped that happen." If she had said she was hungry, Trena added for good measure, she would have told the girl to hop in the car and taken her to get something to eat.

I did see Trena's point, but I still disagreed.

"What she does with the money is between her and God," I said. "I'm not going to disrespect her or God." Maybe I had paid for her drugs that day. But maybe that kept her from selling her body for the money. Maybe that prevented someone from getting HIV. I didn't know. I never would. My role, as I saw it, was to give. Not to judge. I'd been judged.

Maybe I saw the ghost of myself in all of them—the baby whose cries deserve to be heard, the little girl at the cash register resigned to having what she wants snatched away, the young parolees who piss away their own futures, the crack whores hustling in the aisles of church. Something pushes me to step into instead of away from their pain and anger. I'm not fool enough to think I'm there to save them. I just know I can't do that one thing that caused more hurt and damage in my life than poverty, crime, or substance abuse combined: I won't just turn my back and abandon them.

WHEN TRENA AND I HEARD THAT BABYFACE WAS GOING TO BE PLAYING IN CONCERT at the Civic Center in Poughkeepsie, we bought front-row seats to see him. He'd always been "our" singer since I pressed that CD on Trena after we first met and urged her to listen, because his lyrics were my love letter to her. We had dinner at home, then got dressed up and headed out for our big night. Once we were inside the Civic Center, Trena headed off to the ladies' room before we got seated. As I stood there waiting for her, idly watching the crowd heading into the concert hall, a face I instantly recognized emerged. The man walked up to me to say hello and introduce me to his girlfriend just as Trena reappeared. I could tell she couldn't place the couple.

"Trena, you remember, this is Anthony," I said. I could feel her body tense next to mine, and her voice was cordial but her eyes cold as she politely said hello and how are you. "Enjoy the show, man," I said as Anthony Wise excused himself and went to find his seat. I had heard he was out of prison; his sentence for killing Mary King was over while I was still serving time for the murder I'll always believe he and his brother got away with.

"Let's go," Trena said. She was rattled. "Why did you have to bring that guy in front of me?" she demanded. But seeing Anthony Wise didn't mean a thing to me, and I wasn't about to sacrifice front-row seats to Babyface because he was somewhere in the concert hall enjoying the same music. Trena didn't understand that we *had* to acknowledge each other, play it straight, keep it moving. Prison code. If I ignored him, I became a threat, an enemy who was waiting for the chance to jump him. Our charade of civility is what kept it neutral, what let us both just continue on with our own lives.

COMING UP ON THE SECOND ANNIVERSARY OF MY RELEASE, I got astonishing news: I was a finalist for ESPN's prestigious Arthur Ashe Award for Courage. Named for the inspirational tennis champ, the award honors recipients for "possessing strength in the face of adversity, courage in the face of peril and the willingness to stand up for their beliefs no matter what the cost." Past winners included Nelson Mandela, Pat Tillman, and Muhammad Ali. I had gotten on ESPN's radar when filmmaker Jose Morales began filming a documentary on my case for the network after hearing about me from the Innocence Project. When the call came telling me I was the 2011 Arthur

Ashe winner, it was like a gift from God, the one thing my prosecutors and persecutors had withheld from me even in the shameful face of their defeat the day I was freed: vindication. Standing at the awards ceremony in my suit and tie, hearing the crowd applaud and cheer for me, was both my proudest moment and my most humbling.

It had rankled me, the D.A.'s refusal to acknowledge any wrongdoing—or my innocence—even after all the evidence Ross uncovered made my conviction collapse like a house of cards. Who was accountable for twenty-six years stolen from a man's life? Ross prepared a civil suit against the Dutchess County district attorney's office and the Poughkeepsie Police Department, demanding $26 million in damages for what he described as the "gross violation" of my constitutional rights that led to my false arrest and conviction. WilmerHale once again took on my fight entirely pro bono, and Ross and his team dug in for another long haul. It could be years, he warned me. And, just as it had been in my two murder trials, my character would be attacked. What was my life worth? That's what it seemed to come down to. Ross tracked down trainers and boxers who had seen me fight on Sing Sing's boxing team to get expert analysis of my skills and what my potential had been. If I had been free to pursue the boxing career I was just beginning when I got locked up, what could my winnings have added up to over a lifetime? Would I have become a champ? Would I have had endorsements? Would I have left the ring to become a successful manager or promoter? Would I have opened my own gym, or a chain of them? My lawyers had their own complicated calculus for setting damages. I had my own.

No one can ever repay you for a stolen life.

14

"**FAILURE IS A CHAIN REACTION.** So is success." When I repeat those words to a classroom full of at-risk kids, or to a ballroom full of corporate executives, I want them to know that it's not just some generic motivational quote. It's a truth that I know in my heart and have experienced intensely all my life. Even so, winning the Arthur Ashe Award set off a chain of events that I could never have predicted. Here I was, a man past fifty, fully realizing my dreams for the first time.

The Ashe Award generated interest in me as a motivational speaker, and Ross and Shauna set me up with an agency that began booking me for all-expense-paid business trips across the country, and even internationally. Trena and I started a magnet collection on our refrigerator door: Chicago, Houston, New Orleans, Kalamazoo, Australia, even London. I had never flown before and was as excited as a kid to even be in an airport. I didn't have a fear of flying, but going through security gave me flashbacks. If something beeped, I would start shaking.

"I don't know what else I got," I said the first time it happened, turning to Trena for help.

"Babe, take off your belt," she calmly told me.

At the Ashe awards ceremony, ESPN had broadcast a short video chronicling my journey, narrated by actor Matthew McConaughey. The big auditorium fell still at the conclusion, when McConaughey told viewers that I still prayed "to get back one small one piece" of the life taken from me: "He wants just one fight as a free man." One of the people touched by my story turned out to be Dan Beckerman, a senior executive with Anschutz Entertainment Group, the largest owner of sports teams and sports events in the world. Beckerman immediately fired off an e-mail to boxer Oscar De La Hoya, and within days, the two had arranged for my biggest dream of all to come true: I was going to step into the ring as a pro boxer. De La Hoya's Golden Boy Promotions was offering me a spot on the undercard of a light-heavyweight championship match at the Staples Arena in Los Angeles. I had barely three months to get my boxing license and train for the October 15, 2011, match against Larry Hopkins. I had already been helping train aspiring young boxers at my friend Ray's gym, and now it was time to focus intensely on myself. I was proud that with self-discipline and demanding workouts, I had managed to keep my fighter's physique over the years, but a lifetime spent on concrete floors and prison bunks had taken a toll on my back and hips. Watching me do squats or jump rope at the gym, nobody would guess I was in pain. But at home, just getting up from the kitchen table or walking stiffly around the apartment was difficult. It worried Trena, who badgered me about seeing an orthopedist.

"I can deal with it on my own," I told her.

No one over the age of fifty had ever earned their pro boxing license in California, and I would have to pass a whole raft of mandatory medical exams before the state Athletic Commission would decide if I was fit to fight. I was excited to get things moving. Trena and I were up well before dawn to catch our five-hour flight to Los Angeles. "Rock 'n' roll," I told her as we headed from the airport straight to a day full of doctor's appointments without even stopping to unpack at our hotel. I would have to undergo a neurological exam, an MRI brain scan to make sure I hadn't suffered any previous cerebral hemorrhaging, an eye test, a basic physical, blood tests to rule out HIV and hepatitis, and an EKG.

"How many fights do you think you've had altogether?" the neurologist asked, shining a tiny flashlight into my eyes and tracking their movement.

"Ten," I said.

"Ten fights in prison," he repeated.

I nodded. My last one had been maybe fifteen years ago. Was I being a fool to think I could go pro now, even for a single night? Lying on the cold EKG table with electrodes attached to my chest, I remembered the closing line Matthew McConaughey had narrated in my minibiography at the Ashe ceremony: "It'll be easy to train for, considering he's already won the most difficult fight he'll ever face."

Electrocardigram over, I sat up and gave the cardiologist a smile.

"That's a good heart, right?" I prodded.

"Yeah, very good," she agreed.

Next, I met up with Sid Segovia from the California Athletic Commission at a fighters' gym in downtown L.A., where I would be put through the paces. Dressed in a neatly tucked red polo shirt with a state emblem on the pocket, Segovia was every inch the bureaucrat as he consulted the clipboard in his hands.

"Okay, so you're going to do five minutes on the jump rope,

five minutes on the heavy bag, five minutes on the speed bag, then five minutes on the mitt."

Segovia handed me a jump rope and hit his stopwatch. Twenty minutes later, a sheen of sweat covering my torso, I sat down on the edge of the ring, glad it was over. I couldn't wait to get to the hotel. Between traveling, medical tests, and now this, it had been a grueling twelve hours without rest or a proper meal. I just wanted to shower and crash for a while, then maybe go out for a nice dinner with Trena.

"Okay, now you're going to do three three-minute rounds of sparring with Mr. Carthron," Segovia instructed, gesturing toward a young pro-heavyweight named Andrae Carthron who was gloved up and waiting for me. I was dumbfounded.

"I do all that work and you want me to go out there and spar with that man for ten minutes?" I objected. "I've been up since three this morning!"

"Correct," Segovia said in his pleasant robot-official voice. "Again, we're just doing what we were told to do, which is to come here and do an evaluation. We're following the same protocol we do with every athlete in California."

I had my doubts that every athlete flew across the country, underwent hours of medical exams, and then was rushed right into the evaluation of skills all on the same day—while jet-lagged and operating on just a few hours' sleep. I took a long drink of water and breathed deeply to clear my head. *It is what it is,* I told myself. The same mantra had pulled me through far worse challenges than this.

"Okay," I told the evaluator. "Let's go."

"Try not to hurt each other, but we gotta see some skills," Segovia advised us before we began. The bell rang and we went at it. I didn't notice Trena scowling behind her sunglasses on the sidelines, or see her walk out with the kind of ladylike, contained fury that spells serious trouble for whoever set her off. She would later tell me she couldn't bear to watch because it seemed so unfair to her.

The three rounds passed in a blur. I looked at Segovia expectantly. He consulted his clipboard.

"Cardio looked good, technique looked good," he offered. "In terms of how you rated from 1 to 10, that will be determined by our office in Sacramento."

I was dog-tired but optimistic as Trena and I headed to the hotel.

"I believe 99.9 percent that I proved myself," I told her. "I'm this close, this close to getting my fight."

BACK HOME IN BEACON TWO DAYS LATER, THE PHONE RANG. Che Guevara, the California athletic inspector, introduced himself on the other end. He said he wanted to read a letter to me. I was ready to jump out of my skin from nerves. Trena and I put the phone on speaker and listened expectantly.

"Dear Mr. Bozella," Guevara read out loud, "this letter serves as notice that your professional boxing application is currently denied . . ."

I was stunned. My heart fell a thousand feet and broke. I could barely hear Mr. Guevara reading the rest of the letter over the sound of blood roaring through my ears. Trena sat forward in her chair, listening intently while I shook my head in disbelief.

" . . . based on your performance and evaluation process at Strong Sports Gym in Los Angeles. Despite receiving high cardiological reviews, it was the actual sparring session of the eval that raised concerns, Dewey. It was reported that you had difficulty with lateral movement in the ring and it was noted that you showed questionable reflexes and lacked adequate defensive footwork.

"This isn't the be all and end all," Guevara went on, unaware that I had walked out of the apartment, desperate for some fresh air. Trena stayed behind to hear him finish. "You have the opportunity in the next month to hone your craft more, work on some of the things we just listed off, and possibly come back another time to try to make it for your scheduled bout October fifteenth, if that's something you'd like to do."

Guevara waited for me to answer, and Trena improvised.

"Uh, Dewey just went to the men's room," she said. "This is his wife, Trena Bozella."

"Is he okay?" Guevara asked.

"I hope so," Trena said. She had no idea whether I'd gotten into my Honda and driven off in anger or what. In truth, I was sitting on the stoop growing more bitter by the second.

"All that work for nothing, man. All that work for nothing," I muttered to myself. "That's the way my life's been. Always a struggle and conflict. The fuck I'm gonna try it again for? It's over with, man. They killed it! It's over with!" I got up to go back inside.

Trena was still talking to Guevara.

"I know the first part is stunning, probably, to Dewey," he was saying, "but the last portion, we gave him hope. We gave him some avenue to hone his skills and be reevaluated. We're confident that we came up with the correct evaluation in that, at present, he doesn't show the ability to be at that level."

Trena was heartbroken, too, but stayed levelheaded and diplomatic. She had cut through the mumbo jumbo to the heart of what she knew mattered most: I still had a chance. They were willing to leave the door open and let me try again in a month.

"I do believe you didn't get the best out of Dewey," Trena said, "and I believe it's fair that he come on fresh, and then if it still has the same outcome, then I believe it was a fair decision."

Guevara said the letter would explain exactly what I needed to work on. I interrupted before he could read it all over again.

"Where is that fair?" I shouted. How was it fair that I came into the sparring match from a twenty-five-minute workout against an opponent who hadn't had to do the same exercises? "He sat there the whole half hour I worked out! And then you put me with a heavyweight when I'm a cruiserweight. He got me by at least twenty-five pounds!" I was pacing our tiny living room now, stalking back and forth, gesturing wildly at the voice on the speakerphone.

"If you didn't take the advantage away from me, I guarantee you, it's a whole different fight! I probably would've dropped him! But how can I drop him if you take away my energy? He even said, 'Yo, man, you want me to go out and fight this man, spar this man after all the work you did with him?' And you all said go out there, and that's exactly what I did. He didn't beat me, I beat him!"

Guevara was shouting at me now, trying to stop the tirade.

"Dewey! Dewey!"

I kept on bellowing.

"It hurts, man. It hurts! You're taking away my dream. You're taking away the only thing I got left and you killed it!"

Guevara jumped in again.

"Trena? Trena, are you on the phone?"

"Yes, I am," she answered.

"Okay," the inspector said, sounding agitated. "He needs to settle down right now."

Trena pursed her lips. She didn't appreciate being treated like the mother of a bratty toddler instead of the wife of a deeply wounded man.

"Okay," she said tersely. "I appreciate your time."

They hung up, and she turned and tried to get through to me.

"They're going to give you another chance," she said.

"It's over with," I said fiercely.

"Nope." Trena shook her head adamantly.

"Trena, I'm not talking about it no more," I declared. This was it, the end of that road. I wasn't budging.

"Nope," she said again. "You can't quit now."

"It's not quitting. It's reality. The reality is they're going to do the same thing over again."

"The reality is this, Dewey: Nothing ever comes easy for you! That's reality!"

"I'm tired of it, Trena. I'm sick of it."

"Nope. You got thirty days."

"For what?" I hollered.

"Thirty days to find a trainer . . ." she started, but I cut her off again. She shouted over me. "That's how it is! Remember you said you either lie down or you get up and fight? Which one you gonna do?"

"It's not lying down," I argued. "It's just the simple fact they don't want me to fight."

"PROVE THEM WRONG!!" Trena urged. "YES! You're my husband who says never give up!"

"I'm not giving up," I protested. "I'm just pissed."

"Well, pissed ain't going to do it," she said.

"Every single time, it's struggle and conflict, Trena. Struggle and conflict, struggle and conflict, struggle and conflict."

"That's life!" she reminded me.

"I always gotta bust my ass to prove something." My arms were still crossed tight against my chest, but I could feel myself surrendering to her unwavering faith in me, her pure passion for a dream that wasn't even her own.

"That's right," she said, and with that, without saying anything, we knew it was decided. I would try again. There was no way this woman was going to let me sag against the ropes in self-defeat. Not when I was devoting my life to kids who reminded me of what I once had been, telling them every chance I got to never give up, to never let anybody take away their dreams.

WHEN WORD OF MY FAILURE TO GET LICENSED REACHED OSCAR DE LA HOYA, he redoubled his efforts to make a total stranger's lifelong dream become reality: he invited me to train in Philadelphia with Bernard Hopkins, whose match against Chad Dawson was the marquee draw of the Staples Center event. Raised in the tough projects of Philadelphia, Hopkins had grown up on the streets and had run wild from an early age. He was mugging people at thirteen, and when he hit seventeen, he got locked up on nine felonies. He spent nearly five years in the state penitentiary and, like me, turned his life around with boxing while behind bars. I admired his reputation for discipline and clean living. He was living proof that motivation and talent, not age, determined when a fighter was out of the game. Hopkins was just a couple years younger than I was, and at forty-six, he had broken George Foreman's record to become the oldest pro boxer ever to win a world championship. A former middleweight champ who successfully defended his title a record twenty times, Hopkins had changed weight classes to become a prize light-heavyweight fighter later in his career. If there was anybody who knew exactly what it would take—inside and out—for me to prove myself pro material, it was Bernard "The Executioner" Hopkins.

His assistant trainer, Danny Davis, was charged with sizing me up the first day I reported to the Joe Hand Boxing Gym in Philly. A young former Golden Gloves titleholder, Danny had honed a national reputation for himself by training Hopkins into a world-class fighter. Pro athletes, even outside the boxing world, wanted to be at the top of their game.

That first morning, Danny wasted no time in pushing me to my limits. He figured I was done for when it was time for me to work the mitt with him after he had put me through a punishing series of eight exercises that had left me drenched in sweat and panting.

He was wrong.

But I was tired and sluggish. "Too slow, too slow!" Danny shouted as I hit sloppily at the padded target. We broke after two rounds, but I barely had time to gather my strength before Danny ordered me back into the ring for another two rounds. I knew I still had to prove myself, to show him I wasn't some old wannabe who was getting handed a damn pity fight because life had dealt me a lousy hand. Willpower is any athlete's greatest strength, and when I drew on mine, I could feel my body respond with the surge of adrenaline I needed. I was in my zone now, loose and dancing on my toes. Danny noticed. When we finished, he had a big smile pasted across his face.

"We're gonna make some noise," he promised.

I had thought I knew how to train from the books I studied at Sing Sing and from the other boxers and mixed martial arts guys I met in prison. Danny's routine showed me that I was way off. He and Bernard Hopkins at Joe Hand strove not only to condition boxers physically, but to educate them and teach them an art. Before Hopkins recruited him, Danny had worked as a mental health tech in a juvenile facility after he hung up his gloves, and a big part of why he agreed to come on board at Joe Hand was because the owners of the gym made a big commitment to helping at-risk youth. There was even a computer lab for the kids who hung out at the gym or trained after school. Seeing how the people at Joe Hand integrated boxing with building character in these young boys motivated me to stand back up like a man and make it happen in California. The more successful I became, the better my chances of realizing my own dream of opening up a gym like Joe Hand's to help keep kids off the street back in New York.

Sparring was the biggest hurdle I had to face before trying for my license again. "They need to see action," Danny reminded me when I climbed into the ring at Joe Hand. "Put the pressure on him; I want you to make his ass fight," he urged my sparring partner. He came at me hard from the first second. "Keep up the pressure, pressure him, pressure him!" Danny shouted from the sidelines. "Too slow, too slow!" he hollered at me. We took our one-minute break. "Okay, this is the round I want to see him get through," Danny instructed my opponent. "You're gonna make him or break him." We went back for another three minutes. Danny rode me hard. I wasn't pushing back hard enough, my feet were lead. "You ain't gonna pass the test like that!" Danny taunted. I needed to get up on my toes and dance. My opponent pummeled away, backing me up against the ropes.

"Make him box his way out of that corner!" Danny commanded.

I fought my way back to the center of the ring. Danny called time. We both felt good about the progress I'd made. I left Philadelphia stronger and wiser, grateful that Bernard and Danny had compressed their world of experience into just a few weeks. Even if California said no again, I would know for certain now that I gave 100 percent.

I could live with that.

THIS TIME, I ARRIVED FOR MY EVALUATION FRESH AND ENERGIZED. Oscar De La Hoya came to offer his personal support. I knew he had shown up for other reasons, though: he needed to see for himself if I was worth it, because his reputation was on the line as president of Golden Boy Productions. Even though my scheduled fight with Larry Hopkins (no relation to Bernard) was fourth on a nine-fight card, it was already generating a lot of national media interest. Jose Morales and his camera crew had been following me for six months filming their ESPN documentary. Major news outlets like the *New York Times,* the Associated Press, and the *Los Angeles Times* had all written about me. The match, and the story behind it, was going to have an audience that was much bigger than the fans in the Staples Center on fight day.

"I don't wish for the commission to focus on the power of his punches or his speed," De La Hoya explained to the ESPN camera. "I want them to focus directly on his heart, and think about what he's accomplished and think about what he's been through to be right here today. It doesn't get any tougher than that."

This time, I sailed through the whole evaluation process and barely broke a sweat. I dominated all three rounds of the sparring test, and afterward, Commissioner George Dodd pulled me aside. "Let's go talk real quick," he said. I felt a flash of dread. Maybe this was all just a cruel cosmic joke, and California had no intention of licensing a fifty-two-year-old man. It was this guy's job to let me down easy, tell me thanks for trying, go have a great life. He offered a short critique of my jabs, then started gathering up his paperwork.

"You're ready to go," he said.

It took a second for his matter-of-fact announcement to sink in.

"You giving it to me?"

"You got it," he confirmed.

I couldn't wait to share the news with Trena.

"I passed the physical. They gave me my license," I told her. They said I couldn't do it, but I did it. I heard Trena give a little whoop and laugh with joy. I was officially a professional boxer, and my debut was just sixteen days away. There was no time to bask in my sense of accomplishment. I still had a fight ahead of me. My fight.

BACK HOME, I STUCK TO DANNY'S REGIMEN. He had whipped me into top shape, and I had to maintain that training. This time, when we boarded the plane for Los Angeles, it felt like every possible emotion was ricocheting through me at once. I was confident and terrified at the same time. So many people had invested their talents, their time, and most of all, their faith in me. My wife, my legal team, ESPN and ESPYs producer Maura Mandt, Oscar De La Hoya, Bernard Hopkins, Danny Davis, and the other trainers at Joe Hand

Gymnasium. I couldn't bear the thought that I might let any of them down.

Three days before my fight, I was told to stand by the phone for an important call from a supporter: the president of the United States. How was that even possible? Barack Obama wanted to speak to *me*? An ex-con who didn't even have the right to go into a voting booth? The phone rang.

"Dewey?"

"Yes, is this Mr. President?" I asked, even though the voice was unmistakable.

"Yessir! How are you?"

"Oh my God." I was in a state of total disbelief. Sitting next to me, Trena was about to burst. "I'm good," I managed to answer.

"I heard about your story and wanted to call and say good luck with your fight," the president went on. "Everything you accomplished in prison and what you've been doing since is something I think all of us are very impressed with.

"You're certain that there's going to be just one fight you're going to fight?"

"Yes, absolutely, man," I said.

"All right, man. Well, I wish you all the best. Take care."

I told the president to take care, too, said good-bye, set the phone down, put my head in my hands, and rubbed away the tears. I looked over at Trena and shook my head.

"Talk about pressure," I said softly.

OSCAR HELD A PRESS CONFERENCE BEFORE THE FIGHT TO INTRODUCE ME. I knew what the reporters, what the world must have been thinking: I was a nobody freed from prison after twenty-six years trying to realize the dream of my stolen youth. I stepped up to the podium and leaned into the mike.

"I want everyone to know this wasn't just handed to me," I said. "You may think this is charity. This is not a charity thing. I'm out here to win, and I'm going to give you a zillion percent of what I've got at fifty-two, and I'm not busted."

I paused to remove my cap and peel off my shirt, offering my bare chest and six-pack to the cameras.

"I'm not busted! I'm not busted, so I earned mine."

Larry Hopkins had three fights but no wins coming into our match and was considered to be a weak opponent by the boxing press. But I had no pro fights, no wins, and an extra thirty years of wear and tear on my body, so I was still the underdog. When Hopkins saw me before the bout and asked to pose for a picture, I figured it was a psychological ploy to throw me off, mess with my head, make my brain think "friendly" when I saw him again in the ring. *You're not fucking with me,* I silently cursed him while I obligingly smiled for his selfie.

The Staples Center had a decent turnout—more than eight thousand fans—but I felt like it was just God and God alone watching as the announcer drew out my name—DEWEEEEY BOZELLLLA!!—and I climbed into the ring, into the lights. I shrugged off the silk cape emblazoned with my professional moniker, "Radar" Bozella. "Radar" was a twist on "Rader," the middle name I shared with the father whose cruelty had nearly destroyed me. That hurt little boy stepped into the ring, too. The bell rang, and I began to fight.

Hopkins came at me with good jabs, but I could see he was awkward. I wasn't loose and kept throwing sloppy jabs myself as I tried to figure him out. I knew I wasn't crisp. I kept throwing short, giving Hopkins the chance to step in and connect. He threw wild, looping rights from his knees, and I kept my head moving, but a couple still nibbled at me. The first three-minute round ended, and I felt like I was getting a handle on him.

Danny was waiting in my corner. "You all right?" he asked, dressing a small welt over my eye.

"I need water."

Danny spieled off his take on the fight as I drank.

"Relax, relax," he said. "You finished this round off pretty strong. This guy's got nothing. Use your jab a little bit more. Keep your hands up. Throw a little bit more punches. You don't have to be careless. We just need combinations."

I went back in for the second round more relaxed, reminding myself to move more and not stand in front of him dancing. He got in a couple of quick jabs and landed a couple of body shots. Hopkins was spending too much energy too soon. I was sure I could wear him out, but I would have to pace myself, too. I took a hook to the head, but got him with an uppercut to the jaw. The ref called time.

"You gotta let your hands go," Danny urged me. "Dawg, listen. That was a better round. You're giving me better jabs, but let this damn right hand go! Let it go, let it go, and come back. Deep breath. You're doing good with the left. That's all he's got is the right. Come back with the hook. Work that right hand. You hit a couple of good body shots and you stop. Work that body!"

"I don't wanna run into nothing wild," I told Danny. He shook his head. That wasn't going to happen. It was time to let any caution go.

I went into the third round throwing left-right combos and hit Hopkins with a couple of hooks. Hopkins tried to land a haymaker and missed, but got me up against the ropes. Big mistake. I turned and pushed him into a worse position. My confidence was surging now, and I relaxed as I felt my body follow suit, growing stronger with every punch. The opposite was happening to Hopkins. His punches felt weaker and weaker, and I could see him slowing down. He was running out of gas, so I started to dance and move around him faster, taking what was left of his energy.

Back in my corner before the fourth and final round, Danny was beaming.

"Take a deep breath!" he commanded. "How we feel?"

"Good!" I answered.

"How we feel?" he shouted again.

"Good!!" I shouted back. And I did. I felt on fire.

"That was a beautiful round," Danny said. "Show your ass off in this round. He's ready to quit. Don't let him back in the fight!"

Twenty seconds into the final round, I was throwing so many punches that the beleaguered Hopkins spit out his mouthpiece. It could've been an accident, sure, but the thing fit fine the first three rounds, and boxers usually spit out their mouthpieces when they're tired and want to stall, since the ref has to call a one-minute break to clean it. When we started again, I got even more aggressive and landed an uppercut. He spit out the mouthpiece again. The crowd was onto him and booed. I waved at them, *Don't worry, I got him.*

With fifty-seven seconds left on the clock, Hopkins spit it out again. I came at him like a dog chasing the mailman. No way was I going to give up, and no way was he going to deliver a thing. Out popped the mouthpiece. This was getting irritating, and the crowd kept booing. The frustration was just fuel for me, and Hopkins could see I wasn't going to let him down easy. It's better to get disqualified than knocked out, though, and with thirty-six seconds left, the mouthpiece came flying out again. "Ref, how much time?" Hopkins asked. The ref schooled him: "Larry, keep your mouthpiece in, keep your mouthpiece in!" I didn't wait for the fight to be stopped the sixth and last time Hopkins spit it out, smashing him with a right cross just as the final bell rang. He sagged against the ropes. The boos turned to cheers, and I heard the announcer's voice boom out.

"Bozella is the hero of the evening!"

My family and friends swarmed me as the judges announced me the winner by a unanimous decision: 39-36, 38-37 and 38-36. I kissed Hopkins on the top of his head and raised my gloves in victory.

Afterward, I faced the press one last time.

"First and foremost, I'd like to thank God for this opportunity. It was something taken away from me as a kid," I said, thinking back on that hungry, unwanted teenager who had once caught the attention of the great Floyd Patterson. Where would that Dewey Bozella be now, if he had gotten to live his life? What fights did he never have, what victories did he never know? Now all I could do was express my gratitude, the deepest gratitude possible, to the people who supported me and gave me this one belated chance. I couldn't, and wouldn't, ask for more.

"This is my first and last fight," I reiterated for their benefit, and for mine.

It was time to move on, to live the life that finally belonged to me, to try to make a difference in a world that is seldom just, or honest, or even kind. My boxing legacy would say what had always been my truth and my salvation: Dewey Bozella was undefeated.

EPILOGUE

I KEEP A RUNNING LIST OF THINGS TO DO AND DREAMS TO STRIVE FOR on the side of the refrigerator. *Love God* is at the top, and everything flows, as I know it should, from there, all in the hungry shorthand of a man with half a life already squandered. *Speaking, Getting Money, Family, People, Learn How to Forgive.* That last one is what people seem to wonder most about me.

Nearly three years after my release, Ross and Shauna received an e-mail from Wayne Moseley, one of the D.A.'s star witnesses against me. He wanted to set the record straight.

"My coerced testimony is what got him convicted," Moseley wrote my lawyers. "I would like it to be known that I was threatened by the District Attorney that if I did not 'play ball' with the District Attorneys [*sic*] office I would be prosecuted for the murder in question. I was told I had to confess to taking part in the murder and that I was with Dewey Bozella in the home of the victim. I confessed to this crime but did not commit it nor did I have any knowledge of this crime. I continued to tell the District Attorney

I had no knowledge nor did I play any part in this crime but he continued to threaten me with the prosecution of it and if I did not cooperate with him he was going to offer the same deal to Mr. Bozella. This is how Dewey Bozella was convicted."

Moseley said the current D.A., Edward Whitesell, had also contacted him to testify against me during my *Brady* appeal, but Moseley had refused and threatened to tell the story of his alleged coercion if he was subpoenaed. Thirty-five years too late, Moseley was stepping forward to tell the truth. "I was as much a victim of false conviction as was Dewey Bozella based on the actions of the District Attorney," Moseley concluded. His logic was as weak as his character. The letter offered no apology. Moseley's buddy and coaccuser, Lamar Smith, vanished in the wind. My WilmerHale team tried to find him, but hit only dead ends. One day when I was visiting a friend at the Poughkeepsie jail, across from my old stomping grounds at Mansion Square Park, I stopped in a convenience store to buy a lottery ticket and was confronted by a man who looked an awful lot like Lamar.

"Yo, aren't you the boxer Dewey Bozella?" he asked. People sometimes recognize me from my speaking appearances or the ESPN documentary about me. I'm always a little on guard when people approach me, though, especially in seedier parts of town. And being that close to the jail, there was always the chance that this was some hood rat who knew someone locked up who had some beef with me or wanted something. Everybody on the street has their hustle.

"Yeah," I said, keeping it neutral while I sized up the stranger. He looked to be in his twenties.

"Yeah, man, I would like to talk to you a minute," he said. We stepped outside for some privacy, and I waited for him to say what was on his mind. The words that came tumbling out of his mouth left me speechless.

"Yo, man, I'm Lamar's son."

And then: "Can I ask you a question?"

"Sure," I said.

"Did my father testify against you?"

I heard an urgency in the kid's voice. He didn't just want to know, but *needed* to know the answer to this painful question. I kept my own emotions in check and replied as calmly and evenly as I could.

"Yes," I said. "Yes, he did."

The kid looked like I'd landed a haymaker straight to his gut.

"My father told me he didn't," he countered, and I could see how much he wanted to believe that. *Fuck you and your mouth full of lies, Lamar,* I thought.

"Well, I hate to tell you, man," I said, "he's your father, but he testified and put me in jail for twenty years to life."

Lamar's son sagged. "Did he really do that? That's messed up!" He asked to take my picture—proof, I assumed, so he could confront his lying father later—and I let him.

Then, not long ago, I was in a club when the friend I was hanging with spotted someone he wanted me to meet. The man he brought back to the table froze when he saw me. It was Lamar. I was just as stunned as he was. Neither of us said a word at first, then Lamar launched right in about my case.

"Yo, man, I don't wanna talk about it," I interrupted, but Lamar kept going on and on. I pulled out a chair and told him to sit down. Lamar sat, still babbling. His words evaporated the second they left his mouth: there was nothing he could ever say to justify what he did to me, no way he could ever make up for the lies that falsely branded me a murderer and got me sentenced not once, but twice, to twenty years to life. I let Lamar talk until my own silence finally seemed to register. I asked him to stand up, and I stood up as well. Looking into his eyes, I could see that he was facing his worst fear in that moment, and it was me. Neither of us had any doubt that I could whip his ass in a matter of seconds. Instead, I put my hand out to shake his.

"You know what, man? I'm going to let this shit go."

I have to forgive, even when no apologies are offered. It's for me, not them.

Both of my two surviving brothers, Michael and Albert, reached out after seeing me on TV. I wish with all my heart that we could become close as brothers, but we all need to do our own healing first. Leon was the only one who knew how to push aside all the demons of the past and just be family. He was the only one who visited me in prison, who made me feel loved regardless of my circumstances. After he died, I got a small lion tattooed on my chest; I couldn't be there to protect Leon the way a big brother should, but now I carry him close to my heart always. The only thread of my lost family I still hold on to is Maurice. The young son of my foster parents called me out of the blue one day. "Geese!" I laughed when I heard his grown-up voice over the phone from Atlanta, where he's got a good career and family of his own now. His folks are gone, and we don't dredge up the bad memories. We keep it Fourth of July happy.

As the people and agencies responsible for my wrongful conviction attempted to bury my legal team with tons of briefs, motions, and other paperwork, my lawsuit slowly made its way through the court system. The longer they stalled, the more costly the fight became, but WilmerHale never blinked. When our attempts to reach a settlement out of court were met with silence, Ross started to prepare me for trial. It would get ugly, he warned. Their key strategy would be to portray me in the worst light possible, tear my character to shreds, and make me too unsympathetic for any judge to believe worthy of restitution. The bottom line was, they were out to prove I was a piece of garbage. Ross would spend years in a paper war with them, filing legal briefs thicker than the New York City phone book. I had my own message to the system inked across my back after I got out. The word *FREEDOM*, dripping with blood, is emblazoned over two clenched fists breaking free from the chains that bind them. A pair of handcuffs lie on the grass below. There is a moon in the scene, too, representing light in the darkest hours.

DESIGN CLOTHES LINE, LIVE TO 90S, GOOD FOOD, OWN A BOXING GYM.

With my one pro fight checked off the list, I decided to focus my energy on my biggest dream of all: finding a permanent place for myself in the boxing world, so I could use my skills and my story to help give struggling young people the direction, discipline, and passion they needed to succeed in life. With help from WilmerHale, I launched the nonprofit Dewey Bozella Foundation and started searching for space to open my own gym in the same hostile streets where I had sometimes slept when my options ran out. The few buildings on the market with the space to accommodate a boxing gym were either too dilapidated to fix up or quickly snatched up by buyers with deeper pockets than mine. More than a year into the search, I was starting to lose hope when my foundation received a windfall offer: the huge old armory in Newburgh—already home to various after-school programs—had more than enough room and was willing to open its doors to us. We could even put up a boxing ring. Summer was just around the corner. We hired an administrator and began scrambling to put together a program. It was happening! It was finally happening! I felt proud and excited. I couldn't wait to meet my future boxers.

The thirty-five kids who signed up were full of the childlike energy and practiced boredom typical of middle-schoolers. I saw a little bit of myself in every single one, straight up. I was eager to jump right in with them, but none of the equipment we'd ordered showed up on time, and I had to fume while the kids went swimming or on field trips that had nothing to do with my vision for the camp. Finally, with gloves, punching bags, jump ropes, and other equipment in place, I gathered the kids in groups of eight for their first training sessions. I spent all of a single morning just trying to show them how to properly wrap their hands while half the boys played mummy and a few slipped out of the gym unnoticed. I had wrapped my own hand more than thirty times in demonstration and was trying to ignore the girl playing rodeo queen with a jump rope by the time the program manager I'd hired hurried in with bad news: my fugitive stragglers had gone and royally pissed off the Armory people by swinging from an indoor soccer goal and then cussing out the coach who demanded they stop. Now all our kids were banned from the soccer field. I confronted the culprits. "If you don't want to participate, then go," I lectured them. "I made that mistake, and it cost me thirty years of my life! It cost me my freedom. You drop out, and you have two choices: you pick yourself up or you go on the street. Don't waste my time."

In prison, time was endless, but now it was slipping by too fast. I looked at all those young faces, those laughing, earnest, goofing, scared faces, and I had to wonder if there was time to catch them, to protect them, to motivate them. We spent the rest of the day working out. I did every squat, push-up, and jumping jack with them even as my aching back and hip screamed in protest. We ended the day practicing jabs, and I taught the kids the art of the fake-out. "You're in an amateur fight and your opponent's up against the rope. He's tired. You look like you're done with him, then sneak up on him. It's never done when you think it is. Don't give up, don't give in. Give more."

The program was so popular that we were able to extend it by two weeks. Then the bottom fell out: the Armory was kicking me out of the big, open space I'd had and into a small classroom in the basement. I couldn't fit the boxing ring I wanted to put up, or do all the training I hoped to. The dream went back on the refrigerator list. *Just as well for now,* I glumly thought. Judge Cathy Seibel had finally agreed that my lawsuit could go to trial and had set a date just a few months away, in January 2015. At the same time, she noted that there was strong evidence in my favor and urged Dutchess County—the sole defendant remaining—to settle the matter out of court. Ross waited for an offer, but none came until the eve of trial. On a Saturday night before the Monday of my court date, the county agreed to pay me a significant amount of damages. They would not admit to any wrongdoing. I accepted. It was time to move on. What happened will live with me until I die, but I can move on.

That said, I'm still trying to find my way in a world that was never open to me, figuring out day by day who I am and where I fit in. Freedom and independence are two different things. I was just a kid when I got locked up; I never really knew what it was like to make your own choices, to build the life you wanted, to belong to yourself. I spend time each day at an old friend's gym, helping out the aspiring young fighters there, but I 'm still hoping for a place of my own. I'll train anyone who's serious, whether they're ten years old or fifty, and maybe the good Lord will let me coach someone to a world championship so I can cross that one off my refrigerator list. Because when everything's said and done, I know I still have some fight left in me.

TELLING PEOPLE MY STORY is the best way I've found to turn bitterness into hope. I was excited when I got invited in June 2015 to Brazil to speak to legislators, police chiefs, and judges about the importance of preserving DNA evidence to prevent the miscarriage of justice. While there I took an afternoon off to try hang gliding for the first time. We trekked up into the mountains to a high ridge, and I had to will myself to go through with it as my guide got me rigged up and led me to the cliff's edge.

Just keep walking, I urged myself. *Don't look down. Keep your head up, keep moving forward, you know how to do that.*

I stepped off the earth and into the sky. All fear left me, and all I felt was free.

ABOUT THE AUTHOR

In 1983, Bozella's life took a dramatic turn when he was convicted of a murder he did not commit. Sentenced to twenty years to life in Sing Sing prison, Bozella maintained his innocence and exhausted every appeal. He was offered more than four separate chances for an early release if he would only admit guilt and show remorse, but Bozella consistently refused to accept freedom under such conditions. Anger at his imprisonment gave way to determination and instead of becoming embittered, he became a model prisoner: earning his GED and bachelor's and master's degrees; working as a counselor for other prisoners; and eventually even falling in love and getting married. Through it all, Bozella found strength and purpose through boxing, becoming the light-heavyweight champion of Sing Sing prison.